ROSS PEROT

My Life & The Principles for Success

Second Edition

TAPESTRY PRESS   IRVING, TEXAS

Tapestry Press
1401 Parkside Dr. North
Wyomissing, PA 19610
610-375-1422
817-307-2388

Printed in the U.S.A.
10 09 08 07   3 4 5

ISBN 1-930819-19-6

Second Edition layout by
D. & F. Scott Publishing, Inc.
N. Richland Hills, Texas

Dedication

This book is dedicated to the thousands of great people I have had the privilege of working with during my business career, and to America's forgotten heroes—*the creators of new businesses.*

- Creating and building new businesses is vital to our nation's future.
- Businesses are like people—they are born, mature, grow old, and die.
- We must create thousands of new businesses each year to provide good jobs for the American people.
- The giant companies that make up the Fortune 500 were once just ideas. *From small acorns mighty oak trees grow!* We must keep planting the seeds to create millions of good jobs in the U.S.A. for the twenty-first century. This is our highest priority.
  Why?
- If our government does everything perfectly, and we do not have a growing, expanding job base:
  - The standard of living will continue to decline for millions of hardworking Americans.
  - We will not continue to have a large middle class.
  - We will not have the tax base to pay our bills.
- The future of our great country is in the hands of people who successfully create new companies.

Contents

Foreword

This book by my father, Ross Perot, began as a tribute to the many individuals who shaped his life as a youth, a tribute to numerous business associates, and a gift to his family; but as I read it again, I realized it contains a powerful message much needed in American business today. Of the many gifts he has given to me, I especially treasure this because its values are enduring. The values passed down by my father are important in today's world and provide a guide to meeting tomorrow's challenges.

In 1988, Ross Perot founded Perot Systems. This company, as with all of my father's endeavors, has as its foundation the core values that he embraces. These values cannot be measured in terms of stock prices, net profit, asset valuation, or a myriad of other financial indicators. These values are immeasurable. However, he has proven that a values-based company will thrive, and that financial strength will be a by-product.

In the short history of Perot Systems, there are countless stories that display our core values in action. I hope to share these with you someday, as they are amazing accounts of how our associates support their coworkers in times of need or personal tragedy. On the business front, a major factor in our rapid growth is our alliance with organizations that share our core values. When your values are the same, the work is easy.

No one can explain these core values and principles of good business like my father. In his gift to friends and family, he has also written one of the best blueprints to the successful pursuit of business—and life—that you will ever read.

As President and C.E.O. of Perot Systems, and as his son, I would like to thank my father for this wonderful gift. I am happy to be able to share this book with you.

Ross Perot, Jr.

Preface

This book can help you become more successful.

Because my experience is primarily in business, I am speaking of success in terms of how to build a great business; but the principles involved are really principles of life. They can be adapted to any field of endeavor.

A business need not be big to be great. Small businesses are the backbone of the American economy. There are approximately 25 million small businesses in the United States, and they employ more than 50 percent of the private work force. This is the very heart of our economy and of our society. We must continually renew and strengthen this resource.

My purpose in this book is to show you that with a lot of hard work and a little luck, your potential for success is unlimited. Some people think that they do not have a chance because they do not have money. At the urging of friends, I have added a brief biography of my early life to demonstrate that, aside from a few lucky breaks, the only special advantages I had were that I had such wonderful, loving parents and that I grew up in a country in which you can control your own destiny.

IF I COULD DO IT, YOU CAN DO IT.

If we *all* lived by these principles, there would be nothing to keep America from being even better in the future than it has ever been in the past.

Ross Perot (signature)

Book

I

My Life

CHAPTER ONE
My Early Childhood

I was born on June 27, 1930, in Texarkana, Texas. The temperature that day was 117 degrees. Dr. Kittrell, my mother's doctor, had gout, and no fans were allowed in the hospital room. My mother never forgot that experience.

My father, Gabriel Ross Perot, grew up in New Boston, a small town in the northeast corner of Texas. His family had migrated from France through New Orleans. They worked their way up the Red River, establishing trading posts along the river. My grandfather established a trading post in New Boston, near the Red River, which later evolved into a general store. My grandfather's gold pocket watch with a Knights of Columbus watch fob is in my office, next to pictures of my father.

My grandfather passed away while Dad was in high school. Although my father was a good student, he had to drop out of high school and work to support his mother. He initially worked as a Texas cowboy and later learned to be a cotton broker, buying cotton from the farmers and selling it to the mills.

My mother, Lulu May Ray, was an extremely intelligent woman. Her ancestors came from Tennessee in covered wagons and settled in Atlanta, Texas. Her dad's father fought in the Civil War and was captured during the war. The front part of his foot was destroyed. He was kept in a prison on an island in the Great Lakes and had to eat rats to survive. After his foot healed, he escaped by swimming ashore. The water was cold and he had to lie in an empty hut for one month. Then, with most of his foot missing, he walked seven hundred miles back to Tennessee.

A few years later, he died, shortly after my mother's father, Henry Ray, was born. One of my treasured possessions is a small gold wedding ring he made for my great-grandmother from a gold coin while he was a prisoner of war. I keep it in my office near my desk. It was obviously a labor of love created during an extremely difficult time.

When my mother's father, Henry Ray, came to Texas from Tennessee, his family brought furniture in a covered wagon, including the bed on which he was born. This furniture is still among the treasured possessions in our family.

My mother could not afford to go to college. Instead, she worked as an accountant and secretary when she was a young lady.

While my father was still a teenager, he raised a cotton crop under the supervision of Mr. Purtle in New Boston. The Purtle family helped Dad raise cotton because they had been friends with his father before he died. They were good friends and good neighbors trying to help Dad take care of his mother and sister.

Growing and harvesting cotton is really hard work. Dad often told the story of taking his bale of cotton to be sold and seeing the cotton broker make a dollar in a few minutes by reselling the bale. That was when he decided he wanted to be a cotton broker, not a cotton farmer.

Dad walked twenty-one miles from New Boston when he moved to Texarkana. This may seem odd today, but was not unusual at that time. He met my mother at a neighborhood dance. They fell in love and married two years later on February 25, 1923.

I grew up during the Depression. We lived in a house that cost four thousand dollars. Our house did not have a washing machine, so my mother washed all of our clothes by hand, scrubbing them on a washboard. Our food was kept cool in an icebox with blocks of ice that were periodically delivered to our house. My dad worked, saved his money, and bought the house only when he could pay cash for it. Throughout my childhood, he taught me never to buy anything on credit. His words were, "Figure out what you want. Save your money, and when you can afford it, buy it." He emphasized that looking forward to buying something was more fun than actually owning it. I later found this to be true, and this lesson has become a part of my business philosophy.

Since it was so hot in the summer, Dad built a small screened sleeping porch in our backyard, about fifty feet away from our house. The sleeping porch had a canvas top, screened sides, and a rough wooden floor. On hot summer nights, we could take advantage of the breezes and the lower temperatures outside the house.

After dark, we would put on our pajamas, turn out the lights, make sure that no one was walking by, and walk across the yard to the porch.

We slept in one room, and it was really fun. It was even more fun when it rained, unless the wind was blowing and water came through the screened sides. There were several occasions when we got very wet. This was not a major problem because it does not rain much in Texas in the summer.

We had to get up before sunrise so that we could get back into the house while it was still dark.

My parents' first child, Gabriel Ross Perot, Jr., died in 1927 of a stomach ailment that could easily be treated today, but could not be treated at that time. He was only three years old, and his death broke my parents' hearts.

During his short life, one of his favorite activities was to go downtown near Gus Kennedy's Shoe Store on Saturday night when a big part of the community would come together and visit on the streets.

The Salvation Army Band would appear during the evening. My brother would dance his heart out as they played "Onward Christian Soldiers" and other Salvation Army hymns. The band members would give him a tambourine to pass through the crowd to collect money.

My sister, Bette, was born on February 24, 1929, sixteen months before my birth. Bette was a special treasure to Mom and Dad because they missed their son so much.

Bette was an outstanding student. Again and again, my teachers would ask, "Ross, why aren't you like your sister?" I would reply, "She is a lot smarter than I am"—and she is. Bette and I have been very close throughout our lives. She has been, and will always be, a role model for me.

No child could have ever had a more devoted mother. She was a small, warm, loving person, but she set very high standards for Bette and me.

My father and I were close. My earliest childhood memories are of spending hours each day with him. Dad and I did something together every day. He was my best friend, and I was his best friend. We had a wonderful relationship.

Bette and I adored our parents. We would never do anything that would disappoint our parents because we loved them so much. They never said, "Do not disappoint us or you will break our hearts." They loved us, they encouraged us, and we loved both of them. Although I was born in the Depression, during difficult times, I was certainly born rich because of my wonderful parents.

Bette and I loved to sit on Dad's lap as he sat in his rocking chair in the evening. Only one of us could get on his lap at a time, so we worked out an arrangement that gave each of us equal time. While one of us sat in Daddy's lap, the other would sit on the floor next to Mother in her little white chair. We still have Dad's rocking chair and Mom's little white chair, and consider them among our most treasured possessions.

We lived in a great neighborhood where everybody knew everybody else and visited each other regularly. Texas, as I have already pointed out, was a very hot place in the summertime. There was no air-conditioning in those days, so we sat outside on the porch. Neighbors would come over and we would visit on the porch.

We had a very interesting neighborhood. The mayor of Texarkana, William V. Brown, lived across the street from us. He had a wonderful family, and we had a lot of fun together.

Our next-door neighbors were Mr. Reagan and his daughter and granddaughter, Mrs. Neef and Ann Neef. They were wonderful people. Ann Neef was a beautiful girl, older than we were, who was very nice to Bette and me. Mr. Reagan worked for the railroad, and his hobby was gardening. He had a beautiful vegetable garden next to our house and he allowed us to work in it with him. He was a great teacher, and he taught us how to grow vegetables.

Bruce Hickerson and my father were good friends. He had a lovely wife and a daughter, Jacqueline. He was a farmer who lived in Index, Arkansas, about twelve miles from Texarkana. They lived in a very modest house and worked hard. He had all the characteristics of a tough, stoic, Texas cowboy. The Hickersons were kind enough to let me spend several weeks with them one summer. I learned a great deal from Mr. Hickerson about the discipline and the effort involved in growing crops and raising cattle.

Living with them was interesting because they had no bathroom. We took our baths in a #3 tub and used an outdoor toilet, an outhouse. These were wonderful people. From Bruce Hickerson, I learned a great deal about life, responsibility, integrity, and business that has helped me throughout my business career.

I had a number of close friends living near me. Charles Smith lived right across the alley. His dad was a doctor.

Temple Webber, who lived half a block away, was another close childhood friend. We went back and forth to each other's homes several times a day. Their parents could not have been nicer or more supportive. They took us to many interesting places, and we had a lot of fun growing up together.

This was the era before television. Rather than sitting around watching somebody else entertain us, we entertained ourselves by visiting with one another and telling stories. Our parents both spent a great deal of time reading to Bette and me.

My mother and Grandmother Ray would play games with us for hours. Their favorite games were Monopoly, checkers, Chinese checkers, and Flinch, a card game that teaches children arithmetic at an early age. I often wonder how many hours of my life I spent playing those games. We loved every minute when we were playing with Mother and Grandmother. Bette would usually win.

Our parents wanted to give us every advantage. When we were six years old, we learned to swim in a swimming pool owned by the Braumiller family. They had built a swimming pool on part of their dairy farm as a business investment. We also swam in Akin Creek, the YWCA lake, and the Boy Scout pool. These were great experiences until polio came along. At that point, our parents felt that it was unsafe for us to be in a public swimming pool and we were not allowed to swim for awhile. They were particularly sensitive about health matters because of the loss of our brother. They later paid the huge sum of $12.50 per month so that we could swim in a pool at a private club.

Speaking of health matters, in my early childhood, sulfa drugs and penicillin had not yet been developed, and any time we got sick we went through the entire cycle—fever drove away the illness. Anyone who has lived through that experience has a deep appreciation for modern antibiotics that cure infections quickly.

My mother was a great dancer. Mom and Dad loved to go dancing. There was a wooden building north of Texarkana called Club Lido. Once or twice a month they would get dressed up and go dancing. Bette and I both remember how beautiful Mother looked and that she made all of her dresses by hand. Grandmother would help her sew them, but when she walked out the door, they looked like they came from a French designer.

Mother taught me to dance when I was four years old. She rolled up the rug on the bedroom floor, turned on the radio, and we danced. Bette and I cherish those memories.

We did not have many toys, because we could not afford them. Our parents encouraged us to make our own toys. We were constantly creating things from scrap wood, paper, cardboard from old boxes, and whatever else we could find. We made up games to play. We even had invisible friends.

One of the most interesting experiences of my childhood was seeing a movie about Thomas Edison's life. After that movie, I came home and tried to invent things for two years. I cannot really describe how excited I was about trying to invent something new. I had to feed and water the horses every day, so most of my "inventions" had to do with automatic feeding and watering. Of course, I did not have the money to implement any of them. You may find it amusing to know that all of those ideas have been implemented in my stable today.

My parents emphasized doing creative things long before medical studies concluded that it is very important for children to be loved and nurtured when they are small. This is because most of the development of the human brain occurs before a child is three years old. Thanks to our parents, my sister and I were in an ideal environment.

Years later, medical research discovered that the creative side of a child's mind develops at a very early age and is similar to a muscle in the human body. If it is exercised vigorously, it tends to be better developed. This is another piece of good luck in my life, thanks to my upbringing.

We bought groceries from the Highland Park Grocery Store, which was owned by the Kaufman family. I clearly remember that our family spent fifty dollars a month on groceries. Believe it or not, fifty dollars a month was enough to provide adequate food for four people at that time. Each time Mother would go to the grocery store to pay the bill, the Kaufmans would give us a sack of free candy. Bette and I really looked forward to that.

It was customary to buy children new clothes for Easter Sunday. There were several years when my parents could not afford to buy me new clothes, so my mother would take some of my older cousins' clothes and alter them to fit me. I never had any feeling of being unimportant because I did not have new clothes. Instead, I felt very important because my mother had given so much time and attention to sewing these clothes for me.

We did not have any money to take vacations. We had a 1929 Dodge, and we would drive around to nearby towns to visit my parents' friends. We frequently visited New Boston on Sundays, where we would attend church and go to lunch with my parents' friends. We would also go to Atlanta, Texas, and visit my mother's relatives. Atlanta was about twenty-five miles away.

My mother's parents, Henry and Elizabeth Ray, lived in Texarkana, and we adored both of them. Frankly, they spoiled us, as grandparents usually do. Grandmother Ray was a tiny little lady about five feet tall. She was warm, kind, and tender. My most vivid memories of her are that I never saw her when she was not busy doing something with her hands—crocheting, knitting, making hooked rugs, or shelling peas. She was always busy. She had very strong moral and religious convictions, and she expected us to be good.

Some of my most treasured possessions are the things that Grandmother Ray made during my childhood. Today, they are framed and properly cared for in my home and in my children's homes. These things include crocheted bedspreads made completely by her hands and beautiful quilts, including the baby quilt she made for my sister and me. Our five children used this same quilt. Each time I look at these things, they bring back happy memories of my childhood.

I especially enjoyed the hooked rugs that Grandmother Ray made by hand. She would take old feed sacks, stretch them on a wooden frame, and draw a pattern for the rug. She kept all of the old discarded woolen clothes from our family. She would cut these clothes into strips and dye them. She would then make these beautifully patterned hooked rugs by hand. These were labors of love that my family will always cherish. Rugs like this mean more than the most beautiful rugs in the world, purchased at the most expensive stores. My sister and I watched her make them and were inspired by her creativity.

Grandmother Ray had very strong convictions about morality and behavior. "How Great Thou Art," sung by George Beverly Shea, was her favorite hymn. She felt very strongly that people should not smoke, and she often said, "If God had intended us to smoke, He would have put chimneys on our heads."

In her later years, *The Lawrence Welk Show* was one of her favorite television programs. For much of the second half of the 1950s, Bette and I knew that we could always find Grandmother at home on Saturday night, watching Lawrence Welk. One Saturday night we stopped by, and the television was turned off.

We said, "Grandmother, you are not watching Lawrence Welk."

She said, "I do not watch him anymore."

We said, "Grandmother, this is your favorite program."

She said, "I do not watch that program anymore."

And we said, "Why?"

She said, "I just heard that he is playing champagne music, and you know how I feel about drinking."

Years later, I had the privilege of meeting Lawrence Welk. I told him this story, and he loved it.

Grandmother and Grandfather Ray later moved to Stamps, Arkansas, about sixty miles from Texarkana. Grandfather managed the general store for the Bodkaw Lumber Company in Stamps. Some of my earliest and happiest childhood memories are of riding to Stamps in the back of their two-door Willis automobile. Bette and I rode in the rumble seat for sixty miles. Nobody had figured out that this was dangerous. Bette and I loved these trips, even though we were exposed to the wind, the sun, and with no seat belts, the possibility of serious injury.

I clearly remember a small sign in Grandmother Ray's kitchen in Stamps saying, "**A place for everything—everything in its place**." She spent her whole life helping other people, and was a beautiful role model of what a good citizen should be. She was so kind, so decent, so positive, and so cheerful. Her death in 1964 was a sad time in my life. Bette, Mother, and I spent a lot of time thinking about what we could do to honor her memory. Bette came up with the idea that since Grandmother Ray was totally committed to the First Methodist Church in Texarkana, the best thing we could do would be to pay the church debt in Grandmother Ray's memory. We did that to honor her.

My mother had a brother, Henry Ray, who was a radio repairman. He was an extremely intelligent, innovative person with a high school education. Henry wanted to learn to fly an airplane, but there were no airplanes or pilots in our area. He read all the books that he could find about airplanes. Then, he built an airplane with a wooden frame. Grandmother helped him stretch cloth over the frame. The cloth was then painted to give it greater rigidity and make it less porous. He bought a World War I engine and installed it in the airplane.

Henry had a problem—there was no one around to teach him to fly, so he took his plane out to a nearby pasture for its test flight. Grandmother insisted on going with him to make sure that he would be safe, and she sat behind him in the open two-cockpit plane. Her instructions to Henry on his first attempt at flying were, "Henry, you fly low and slow." Of course, this is the worst advice you can give a pilot. Fortunately, Henry had read enough about flying to know that much.

He took off without any problem, maneuvered the plane well, and landed successfully. From there, he went on to become an accomplished pilot, and later flew to Alaska and back. Years later, when my son, Ross, was about six years old, he would sit on Henry's lap for hours, flying in his Cessna.

I remember standing in a pasture near Atlanta, Texas, when I was about six years old watching Uncle Henry teach a man named Archie Olds to fly. Archie went into the Air Corps in World War II, became a general, and later became the commanding officer of the Strategic Air Command.

Seeing people like Uncle Henry and Archie Olds—who both had very little in the way of resources—dream great dreams, pursue those dreams, and realize those dreams, really inspired me.

My mother had another outstanding brother named Hutchinson Ray. He died as a young man from undulant fever caused by drinking unpasteurized milk. My mother and grandparents were both seriously wounded by this tragedy.

We called my father's mother Mama Ball, but her real name was Margaret. She was a brilliant woman. Her father, Professor Tisdale Anderson, helped create the public school system in Arkansas. He was a Scotsman. Margaret married my grandfather, and as I mentioned, he died when my dad was in high school. A number of years later, she married Mr. Wade Ball. Mr. Ball later passed away, and she was a widow again. She lived in Texarkana, and she was also a very positive influence on our lives because she was so intelligent and spoke and wrote so beautifully. She set very high standards in ethics, etiquette, and intellectual capability. We always loved our visits with her because she was so interesting and had so many great stories to tell children.

My father's sister was named Oma. She married a young man, Keller Hoffman, who, as an officer in World War I, was exposed to poison gas. He and Oma had two children, Keller,

Jr. and Perot. Keller, Sr. lived for only a few years after the war. His military uniforms were stored at our house, and I remember going through the trunks years after his death, looking at his uniforms and equipment. I learned at an early age that war creates great hardships for the families of those who gave their lives to preserve and protect our freedoms.

My father took responsibility for taking care of his mother, his sister, Oma, and paying the expenses of rearing her boys. He did not have the money to do it, but this was his family, and he just did it. He never said a word of complaint, and my mother never complained once about my dad giving money to his family. She felt it was the right thing to do. He never discussed it with me, but as I watched him over the years, he was a tremendous role model to me in terms of taking personal responsibility for family members.

My sister started to school a year before I did. At first she attended a public school, but my mother was not happy with the quality of the school. Our parents made the decision to send Bette to Patty Hill School, a private school in Texarkana. Miss Patterson operated this school. The tuition was seven dollars a month. This required major financial sacrifices by our parents. The following year I attended Patty Hill School also, and the cost to have two children in school went up to fourteen dollars a month, creating the need for further sacrifice.

One of my earliest and most vivid memories of Patty Hill is my mother driving us to school every day because it was several miles from our house. We only had one car. My dad either walked to his office or caught the bus so that we could get to school. This was another striking indication to Bette and me of how much our parents loved us.

We were required to memorize a Bible verse each day at Patty Hill, and Bette and I did this as we rode to school. Bette memorized the Bible verses quickly. I was constantly looking for short verses. My favorite was the shortest verse in the Bible, "Jesus wept," but that only got me through one day.

As time went on, we memorized the 23rd Psalm and many other longer portions of the Bible and recited them before the class in the school.

Outside my office is a copy of the Aitken Bible. It was printed by our government during the American Revolution, at a time when money was so scarce that our troops were fighting barefoot in the snow. Prior to the Revolution, all Bibles printed in English came from England, and the colonists had to pay a tariff. The reason that the government authorized the printing of the Aitken Bible was because children in schools no longer had Bibles to study. Obviously, the people who gave us our freedom and the Framers of the Constitution had a different view than that expressed in recent Federal Court decisions.

Patty Hill School was located in an old house. The classes were very small, but the teachers were incredibly talented and set the highest standards. Each child had to learn to play a musical instrument. I had to learn to play the accordion, even though I really did not want to. Years later, I read studies about the positive impact that learning to read music and play musical instruments at an early age has on the development of the brain. I realized that I probably would not have had the skills to get a job at IBM had I not been required to play the accordion at Patty Hill School. I had an excellent teacher, Annie Laurie Rehkoph. Even though I was reluctant to learn to play the accordion, it turned out to be a lot of fun.

Beginning in the first grade, each child was required to make speeches. There was a program once a week, in which the children sang, made speeches, and entertained the parents. Several plays were performed each year by the students. In every possible way, this tiny little school, in an old house, was developing the full potential of small children. Patty Hill School was not part of a government program. This was a tiny, private school that was doing incredible things in a little town in the middle of nowhere during the Depression. This is the way America used to work.

I had great friends at Patty Hill School, including George and Rule Beasley, Hayes McClerkin, Bill Murphy, Fred Graham, and Imogene Whyte, who later married Bill Murphy.

Once, the students at Patty Hill School took a one-day train trip to Little Rock, Arkansas, to visit the state capitol. I was really excited because I had never been on a train. We had a terrific time, and as I was riding back to Texarkana, I remembered that my parents always brought me small gifts on those rare occasions when they had been away from Bette and me. When we arrived in Texarkana, I raced to the newsstand at the train station, where they sold gifts, and bought my mother a colored picture of Jesus Christ on the mountain. I bought my dad a leather card case. My mother framed the picture of Christ and hung it in their bedroom. Dad used the leather card case for the rest of his life.

When I was six years old, I really wanted a bicycle. When I told my dad, he looked at me, smiled, and said, "Son, work, save your money, and buy a bicycle." It may seem unthinkable that a six-year-old should work, but during the Depression it was normal. This started my business training.

From that time on, I only bought things I could pay cash for, and I always kept a cash reserve. Initially, I kept money in a fruit jar. Then, I opened a savings account so I could earn interest. During World War II, I bought defense stamps and bonds issued by the federal government to support the war effort.

The first decision I made was that I would buy a second-hand bicycle because it cost less. I sold flower seeds and Christmas cards and made enough money to buy my first bicycle for five dollars. I cannot convey the excitement and anticipation I had during the weeks and months that I was selling things to earn enough money to buy that bicycle. I will never forget the day I bought it, but just as my dad had predicted, three or four days later, it was simply something that I now owned. In fact, it had been a lot more fun to look forward to it than it was to own it. I rode that bicycle on paper routes and other jobs.

We rarely took trips, but in 1936, Texas was celebrating its centennial in Dallas. My parents wanted Bette and me to understand Texas history and attend the Texas Centennial. Again, at great personal sacrifice, they put us in the 1929 Dodge and drove us to Dallas.

We stayed at the Adolphus Hotel. There was no air-conditioning, and it was brutally hot. In the middle of the night, when Bette and I could not sleep because of the heat, my dad took the top sheet off the bed, soaked it in cold water, and laid it over us—a standard Texas technique for getting through a hot night in the '30s.

The next day we went to the State Fair and savored every minute of it. My most vivid memory was seeing all the new cars; and my dream, as we left Dallas, was that someday I would be able to have a car. Years earlier, in the early 1900s, my grandfather, Gabriel Perot, who owned the general store in New Boston, sold cars. They were shipped to his store in boxes. There were no mechanics, so the local blacksmith, who shod horses, assembled and repaired them. The new owners had a problem—there were no roads—so they just drove them around on the prairie. Little did I know that in this great country I would one day become the largest individual stockholder of General Motors—only in America!

While we are on the subject of entertainment, every year the Ringling Brothers Circus came to town. My dad and mother always took us to see the animals unloaded from the train. We watched the elephants help set up the tents. These free events before the circus were better than the circus itself, but our parents also sacrificed to buy four tickets and took us to the circus. It was a really big show!

I especially remember the animal trainers. Clyde Beatty was the most famous animal trainer, and I sat spellbound as he ordered tigers and lions to sit on stools. When I got home, I spent weeks trying to get my dog to do the same thing—with very little success.

On several occasions, my father took me to the Fort Worth Stock Show and Rodeo. We could not afford to stay overnight, so we would get up early in the morning, take the train to Fort Worth, see the Stock Show and Rodeo, and immediately get back on the train to go home. I had about eight hours to visit with him going to and from Fort Worth, and that was even better than the rodeo. Those trips were made at great sacrifice to him, and he did it for one reason. He loved me.

We were surrounded with pets when we were small children. We had a collie and German shepherds. Our collie was named Lassie and our German shepherds were all named Shep. Later, I had a Chinese chow named Chang. I would spend hours sitting on the back porch steps petting the dogs and talking to them. It never occurred to me that they could not understand what I said.

Dad would periodically bring home surprises. One night he brought home a goat. Goats are very intelligent and can be easily trained. The first animal I successfully trained was a goat. He would follow me everywhere and would do all kinds of interesting tricks.

My parents gave us white rabbits on several occasions. They were pretty and interesting to look at, but we were never able to teach them tricks or play with them. I never talked to rabbits. Even I could figure out that they were not very smart.

There was a creek a few blocks from our house that was a great source of pleasure. It was our "Disney World." We pretended to be cowboys and Indians. We played every game in the world. We tried to catch fish, but rarely did. There were many snakes, but fortunately, we were never bitten. Right after it rained, the creek would be quite deep, and we would get inner tubes and float down the creek for several blocks. The fact that we had to create our own entertainment was a very healthy thing that helped us to be creative and innovative.

At one time, we built a teepee alongside the creek. This was a huge project because it took so many poles. We thought it was going to be an easy job, but it turned out to be long, slow, tedious work. After spending several hours inside, it was too hot to enjoy. It just did not work out, but it was an interesting project.

Once a year, we would go to the New Boston County Fair. This was a big event, and we all looked forward to it. Once we got to the fairgrounds, we were surrounded by my father's childhood friends. Looking back on it, my most vivid memory is that my dad would always make arrangements for the two or three black people who worked with him at his office to attend this fair. This was at a time when black people were often treated rudely if they attended events like this. My father would give each one of them his business card and tell them that if anybody was rude to them, to show them his card. He was a person others respected, and they would leave his employees alone.

When these men got too old to work for my father, he continued to pay them. I asked him, "Why do you continue to pay these men?" His exact words were, "Son, these people have families. They are just like us. They need the money."

Sunday, after church, Dad and I would go to their homes and visit with them. He did this because he loved them. He never said that, but it was obvious he did it as an act of love. He sacrificed to make sure they had enough money. Some of my happiest childhood memories are of going to their houses, sitting on their front porches, and having a good visit with friends.

One of the pleasant events that took place periodically in Texarkana was going to Johnny Pecorella's barbershop to get a haircut for thirty-five cents. All the barbers were great characters. Everybody told great stories and had a lot of fun. My dad was one of their favorite customers, because of his sense of humor. Mr. Pecorella was an outstanding man with a wonderful family, and I had many great visits to his barbershop, especially when my dad and I were there together.

Humor was important in getting Texans through the Depression. For example, my dad had a good friend who owned a Greek restaurant. One day, he lost his arm in a serious accident.

My dad immediately rushed to the hospital to donate blood. The Greek restaurant owner recovered, and for years he would tell his friends now that he had Gabe Perot's blood in him, all he wanted to do was try to trade cotton.

On another occasion, a farmer, Joe Paup, was in the hospital. He was very depressed and thought he was going to die. The doctor said he was not and asked my dad to try to cheer him up. Dad went to his room and talked with him for a few minutes. Joe was still very depressed and crying. My father went into the closet, took Joe's coat out, and tried it on in front of a mirror. Joe sat up in bed and said, "Gabe, what are you doing?" He said, "Joe, I am trying on your coat because you are not going to need it if you die." At that point, Joe Paup jumped out of bed and chased my dad out of the hospital, then got in his truck and went home. Another case of Texas humor.

We lived six blocks from the railroad tracks. During the Depression, the freight trains were filled with hoboes, wandering from town to town, looking for work. Every day they would come by our house looking for food. My sweet mother would always give them something. These people were poor and desperate, but there was absolutely no fear that they would ever break into our house. We left the doors unlocked. When they knocked on the door and asked for food, there was no concern that they might break in and steal things. My mother shared our food with them.

One day, a hobo said, "Lady, don't you have a lot of people stopping by here?"

My mother said, "Yes, we do."

He said, "Do you know why?"

She said, "Not really."

Then he took her out to our curb, showed her a mark on the curb, and said, "Lady, you are a mark. This says that you will feed people. That is why you get so many visitors."

After the man left, I turned to my mother and said, "Do you want me to wash that mark off the curb?"

She replied with words that I will remember for the rest of my life—"No, son, leave it there. These are good people. They are just like us, but they are down on their luck. We should help them."

At Patty Hill School, every student was required to memorize these words:

**"Help the man who is down today.
Give him a lift in his sorrow.
Life has a very strange way,
No one knows what will happen
tomorrow."**

And

**"I was angry because I had no shoes,
And then I met a man who had no
feet."**

These things have a lifelong impact on a small child. Unfortunately, the Federal Courts do not allow such principles to be taught in school today.

CHAPTER TWO

Horses, Cowboys, and Jelly Beans

My father was anxious for us to learn to ride horses. Buying a Shetland pony, Patsy, for my sister and me was a huge expense, but he did it and he taught us to ride. We rode Patsy endlessly, and both of us became very good riders.

Dad quickly moved me up to larger horses and even bought a horse for himself. We would ride every afternoon after school. Try to imagine the impact of being with your dad several hours a day as you are growing up—visiting with him as one adult to another. Dad always treated me as an adult. He told me what had happened that day, and he taught me about business. He told me great Texas stories. Contrast this experience to that of children who watch television when they come home from school.

Dad bought a secondhand saddle from Bruce Hickerson's brother, Rob, for thirty-five dollars. It was a Jumbo saddle made by Padgett Leather Company in Dallas, Texas. I was with him when he bought it. He rode on that saddle all his life. Unfortunately, it was sold after his death. Bette and I have looked for it all over the Texarkana area, but we have never been able to find it. I regret this because it had a special place in our hearts.

Maintaining these horses was very expensive. In the cotton business, you have good years and bad years, depending on the weather and cotton prices. I came home one day, walked into the kitchen, and found my mother crying as she was washing dishes over the sink.

She was a strong woman. I had rarely seen her cry.

I ran to her, hugged her, and said, "Mother, what is wrong?"

She turned to me and said, "Son, your dad has sold his horse."

I said, "Why did he do that, Mother?"

And she said, "So that we can afford to give Bette and you a nicer Christmas."

He never said a word about it, but for the rest of my life, I will always remember what he did for both of us. Surely, you can understand why I have said throughout my life that I was born rich.

A farmer named Eli Rochelle lived directly in front of our house. His farm was about twenty miles away. He had several acres of land adjoining his house and rented that land to my father at a very low price. This gave us a place to put our horses. Mr. Rochelle did not have any children, and he would take me with him to his farm during the summer. I would spend the entire day with him. I learned a great deal while at the farm and while visiting with him, as we drove back and forth.

I could break and train horses when I was seven years old. My mother did not like this, but Dad thought it was good experience for a boy. He had grown up at a time in Texas when boys broke horses, and he felt he had learned a lot from this experience. I learned some hard lessons breaking horses. I was thrown many times and knocked out, a 1930s term for a minor concussion. I was brought back to consciousness by having my head put under a water faucet and typically would get back on the horse and ride again. My nose was badly broken many times.

On one occasion as I was regaining consciousness, I saw my dad's face through the water pouring over my head. He looked at me and said, "There never was a horse that could not be rode, and there never was a cowboy that could not be throwed" —more Texas wisdom.

My sister and our neighbors still clearly remember my mother's strong feelings about this activity, and it was one of the few things about which my mother and father disagreed. My dad resolved the problem by not having me break horses when my mother was around.

Over time, I learned a number of techniques to train a horse without getting thrown, and this was a lifelong lesson. Why get bucked off if there is a better way to do it?

Near my desk in my office are some great pictures of my dad riding one of my favorite horses, Candy. There is another picture of a barn that Dad and I built. It was very crude, but it meant a great deal to us and we had a lot of fun building it. Of course, the best part was the hours we spent working together.

One of my boyhood friends was Henry Phillips, whose father was a barber. He was older than I, and he helped my dad and me break horses. We had a number of interesting adventures during this time period, and Henry had a very positive impact on my life. He is now a successful business-man in Georgia.

Two of our neighbors, and my parents' close friends, were Dr. and Mrs. Joe Tyson. Dr. Tyson and my dad had grown up together in New Boston. The Tysons lived two houses away from us on Olive Street. They had two wonderful children, Janet and Joe, Jr. They were younger than Bette and me, but we had a lot of fun playing together.

Dr. Tyson asked me to break a pony that he had bought for his children. He thought the pony was gentle when he bought it, but later found that it was completely out of control. This seemed like an easy job to me because I had been breaking large horses. I took the pony and rode it until it was completely gentle. I brought it back to Dr. Tyson to show him that the pony was ready for his children to ride.

Shortly before I reached his house, I stopped by the grocery store and bought a sack of jelly beans. I ate all of the jelly beans on the way to his house. Dr. Tyson, Mrs. Tyson, Janet, and Joe, Jr. came out to see me demonstrate how gentle the pony was. I ran up behind the pony, put my hands on its hips and leap-frogged into the saddle. The second I hit the saddle, the pony started bucking. I did not have control of the bridle and I did not have my feet in the stirrups. The pony threw me.

Janet Tyson tells a very vivid story of seeing me landing on the ground and being knocked unconscious with a severely broken nose, which was also bleeding.

Mrs. Tyson called my mother. By the time she arrived, I had regained consciousness. But my mother and father had another serious conversation about whether or not I should be breaking horses.

The worst part of this experience was that I was really sick for several days, and I threw up the jelly beans. After the initial convulsion, I continued to throw up for several days. After that, things settled down and life went on. To this day, I have never eaten another jelly bean, and I have never attempted another circus act on a horse. The broken nose almost prevented me from getting into the Naval Academy several years later.

On another occasion, I was thrown high into the air. My dad turned to my sister, Bette, and said, "We may have to send him a telegram to get him down—no need to mention this to Mother."

One day my dad came home with a pair of cowboy chaps made for a boy my size. I thought it was the greatest gift in the world. I used them in the rodeos and any other time I rode. Those chaps are now framed, and each time I look at them in my home, I think of my parents.

Another unique gift my father gave me was a pair of spurs he bought for three dollars at a fire sale. I kept them for years and used them while my children were growing up as we rode horses. One day they just disappeared. We have turned the earth upside down looking for them, and I would give anything to have them back even though they only cost three dollars.

I have learned lessons from some very interesting people. Harvey Rivers was the blacksmith who shod our horses. He taught me how to keep horses under control, and I would always look forward to my visits to his blacksmith shop. When I got older, Dad would have me ride one horse and lead our other horses to have their shoes replaced. Riding through traffic with horses tied together by halters and ropes was quite an adventure. It was tricky getting across the New Boston Road. It was even trickier getting across Seventh Street at the intersection where Dunbar School was located. I would finally arrive at Harvey Rivers' blacksmith shop, which was within sight of the most infamous house of prostitution in Texarkana—711 West Fourth Street. Of course, this had nothing to do with getting horses shod, but my mother was a little sensitive about my even being in that area. I would be in Mr. Rivers' shop for several hours, and he told me a thousand good Texas horse stories. He would tell me practical ways to cure horses when they were limping. It was a great experience.

My dad had a number of friends who were Texas cowboys, including Melvin Hudson and Hub Whiteman. They both had ridden and competed in the world championships in Madison Square Garden during the time when real cowboys rode in the rodeos.

I participated in local rodeos as a young boy doing trick and fancy roping. My dad had taught me how to spin ropes, and I became quite good at it.

I would occasionally do a special event in small-town rodeos, because I was a good calf roper. I had to ride a full-size horse to rope a calf. I was too small to get on the horse so they had to put me on the horse, and I was certainly too small to throw the calf and tie it after I had roped him, so my event was simply coming out of the chute and roping the calf. The crowd would get all excited because a little boy could rope the calf.

From the time I was about ten years old, my dad would take me to the horse, cattle, and mule auctions every Friday at the Owen Brothers barn. He began teaching me the fundamentals of trading by letting me buy and sell inexpensive bridles. My goal was to buy a bridle at one price and sell it at a higher price, but he required me to sell everything the same day that I bought it. This was referred to as day trading. In other words, we never took anything home. He was teaching me how to make a profit and how to negotiate. He soon allowed me to buy and sell saddles, which were more expensive, but again only as a day trader. Finally, he allowed me to start buying and selling inexpensive horses. Once again, I would have to buy and sell them on the same day. This was my Ph.D. in business, taught at my father's knee.

CHAPTER THREE
A "Roads" Scholar

I mentioned earlier that I sold Christmas cards and garden seeds when I was six years old. I have said all through my life that these were my Harvard Business School experiences.

Years later, after our computer company, EDS, was financially successful, I was riding up a chairlift in Vail, Colorado, and the person next to me said, "Ross, Vail is for sale. Do you want to buy it?"

I replied, "No, I am not interested."

He asked, "Why not?"

I replied, "When I was six years old, I learned not to get into a seasonal business."

He said, "What do you mean?"

I said, "I sold Christmas cards and garden seeds, and they were good businesses for a brief period of time. I want to be in a year-round business." I thought he was going to fall out of the chair laughing.

I also sold the *Saturday Evening Post* magazine throughout our neighborhood. Knocking on our neighbors' doors and trying to sell them a magazine was a great experience. Norman Rockwell's paintings were on the covers. After becoming successful in business, I collected Norman Rockwell paintings. Surely, the reason is obvious.

My parents installed a huge fan with blades almost four feet in diameter in the attic of our house when I was eight years old. It pulled fresh air through open windows into our house during the summer, and we no longer needed our sleeping porch. This was a really big event. These fans were called attic fans.

Every Sunday, unless we were on our deathbeds, we were in Sunday school and church. This was a must in our family. We attended the First Methodist Church in Texarkana. It had a wonderful congregation of people who were closely knit together as friends. During tough times like the Depression, people's religious convictions are strengthened.

Again and again, it was hammered into all the little children in Sunday school to follow the Golden Rule, to be good neighbors and to live according to the teachings of the Bible. Following Sunday school, we got another hour in church.

After church, we would have dinner at Bryce's Cafeteria, owned by the Lawrence family. We called our noon meal *dinner* and our evening meal *supper*. The food was great, and the visits with our friends were even better.

My father grew up in the Catholic Church because his dad was Catholic. After marrying my mother, he became a Methodist. He and Father O'Brien, the Catholic priest, were good friends.

Max Sandberg and Joe Eldridge, two of my dad's good friends, were Jewish.

There was a black church in Texarkana named Polly Chapel Church. My dad loved the choir in this church and would take me to the services. When his friends in the black community were being baptized, we would attend the ceremonies. These services took place in ponds and lakes around Texarkana. These were wonderful experiences that I will never forget.

At a time when many people were rigid about racial and religious differences, my parents made it clear to Bette and me that the important thing was to believe in God and that your specific race or religion should not be an issue.

The fact that we grew up with people of different races and religions and had close associations with them had a significant impact on our lives.

From time to time, the Red River would flood, flow over its banks, and tear out the levees. The farmland would be devastated. These farmers were my father's friends and customers. He would immediately go visit with them. Some of my most poignant childhood memories are of standing at the edge of the water as it raced across the farmland. The barns had been destroyed, mules and cattle had been swept away, the crops had been destroyed for the year, and yet the farmers and their families were standing there stoically. Nobody complained— nobody cried—this was just nature. They knew the river would go down and they would farm again. I also remember neighbors helping neighbors rebuild the barns and put things back together when the river went down. This was America at its very finest.

A major event occurred in my life when I was nine years old—I joined the Cub Scouts. We had a great Cub Scout pack. I read all the information and got really excited. My dad was very proud that I had joined the Cub Scouts, and one thing that I will treasure throughout my life is the fact that he bought a Boy Scout knife for me. I believe it cost a dollar. I carried that knife with me at all times, and every time I looked at it, I knew that he must really love me a lot to spend a dollar on a Boy Scout knife.

I learned a great deal from Cub Scouting without realizing it. There were several levels—Bobcat, Wolf, Bear, and Lion— and I decided that I would achieve all of those levels. Without realizing it, I set goals and achieved them for the first time in my life. Our den mother was Mrs. Overholser, the mother of my boyhood friend, Ed Overholser. Our meetings took place in their home. She was a great lady and a wonderful den mother. As Cub Scouts, we were always making things. We did not buy things and play with them. We made things and then enjoyed them.

After completing Cub Scouting, I joined the Boy Scouts. Troop 18 was sponsored by the Morriss family, who owned the Offenhauser Insurance Company. Our scoutmaster was Sam Shuman, who worked for the Offenhauser Company. One of my boyhood idols was Josh Morriss, Jr., the son of the owner of the Offenhauser Company, who lived down the street from us. The Morriss family represented all that is good in America. They were financially fortunate. They even had a tennis court at their home, which was really unusual in Texarkana. They allowed the neighbors to play on their tennis court anytime they were not using it. I never got over the fact, and my parents constantly reminded me, of how wonderful it was that the Morriss family would let anybody enter their property and play on their tennis court. This is what a great, free country should be about—caring and sharing.

I learned that the rank of Eagle Scout could be achieved in thirteen months, so I set a goal to become an Eagle Scout in thirteen months. I accomplished this goal. One more time, I was learning to set goals and achieve them.

I needed to work every summer, and I did. I was only able to go to Boy Scout camp one time for a week, even though the cost was only seven dollars. We had a great adventure at Camp Pioneer in Mena, Arkansas, during that week. In the succeeding years, many of my friends in Troop 18 went to Boy Scout camp Philmont in New Mexico. My dream—my fantasy—was to go to Camp Philmont. I never made it, because I needed to work.

I was eleven years old when Pearl Harbor was bombed and the United States entered World War II. An ordnance depot and arsenal were built between Texarkana and New Boston. All of us were convinced that the Germans would attack these facilities. None of us realized that the German planes did not have the range to fly from Europe to Texas. We had blackouts. We all studied first aid. We were ready, if and when, the enemy attacked.

World War II was a difficult time. Everyone knew someone who was killed in the war. All of us were inspired by their courage and their commitment to our country. During my entire life, I have never seen our country more unified and focused than it was during the war. Our own family was directly impacted. Uncle Henry served in China, and I had two cousins, the sons of my father's sister, Oma, who also served in World War II.

As Boy Scouts, we collected tinfoil, used cans, and old newspapers to support our country. Food, shoes, and gasoline were rationed. These sacrifices were insignificant, but they bonded our nation together.

During World War II, there was a shortage of living space in Texarkana because of the arsenal and the ordnance depot. We had a room next to our garage where we stored saddles and bridles. We also used it as a workshop. My dad and I immediately cleaned out the room, put in a bed, chairs, and furniture, and made it available for military people coming into Texarkana. An army officer lived in that room for several years. This was just one more small thing we could do to support the war effort.

One of the great events of my childhood was when Secretary of the Treasury Henry Morganthau, Jr. came to Texarkana to raise money by selling war bonds. A big event was held, and I was the Boy Scout asked to be his escort. I could not believe that they had asked me.

During the Depression and throughout World War II, my parents spent very little on personal entertainment. Once a month, they would go to a movie at the Paramount Theater. It cost them twenty-five cents each. They always sat in the same seats, so that if Bette or I needed them, we could call the movie theater and find them immediately.

Bette and I would go to the movie from time to time with our parents. The cost was ten cents for children. These were really big events in our lives and we always looked forward to them. The movies were positive and inspiring. The most extreme thing that occurred during my childhood was in the movie *Gone with the Wind* when Clark Gable said, "Frankly, my dear, I don't give a damn." Everyone was outraged. Times have changed!

A constant in our lives in terms of entertainment was to go downtown on Saturday night with our parents, stand on the sidewalk, and visit with all of the people who came downtown, including the farmers who would drive in from the surrounding areas. This was a big weekly outdoor social event that cost nothing, unless you wanted to go to Reason's or Boyd's Drugstores and buy an ice cream cone for five cents.

There were times when things got pretty dull, and we would go to the train station or the Greyhound Bus terminal just to see who was coming through town. It was fairly interesting to sit there, visit with our friends, hear the conductors call out "all aboard," and watch the travelers passing through town—and again, this cost nothing.

As children in Texarkana, we were 100 percent accountable at all times. Everybody knew our parents. If anybody saw us do anything bad, our parents would be called immediately. As my friends and I walked down the street, a thousand eyes were watching us.

I was surrounded by friends, all of whom were more talented than I, and this inspired me. They were the finest students and leaders in our class.

After finishing the fourth grade at Patty Hill, I transferred to the public schools. I skipped the fifth grade because Texas changed from an eleven-year to a twelve-year system, and I entered the public schools in the sixth grade. I became close friends with Jim Morriss, Ed Overholser, and Paul Young.

The following year was my first in junior high school. I made several great new friends who had just moved to Texarkana with their families. A new prison had just been completed, and many federal employees were being transferred from Kansas to staff the prison. Richard Russell and Bill Wright became my close friends. Their fathers both worked at the prison. John

Carnahan, who was also from Kansas, became a good friend. These Kansans were incredibly smart and talented.

One of my closest boyhood friends was Paul Young, who lived near the high school and about a half mile from our house. He is one of the most talented people I have ever met. He was always an inspiration to me, not only because of his intellect, but also because of his leadership ability.

For some reason, Paul and I were preoccupied with digging caves. We would look for a hill made of red clay, and then start digging. This was slow, painful digging. There was always the chance that the ceiling would collapse. We tried to create arches to make it safe. The good news is that it was so difficult to dig these caves that they were not very deep. The great news is that we never had one collapse. After playing in it for a while, things got pretty dull, so we started working on our next cave. Our parents would make us fill in the old cave for safety reasons.

During one of his innovative moments, Paul decided that the best way to make a safe cave would be to dig directly underneath the concrete slab of his neighbor's garage. He and I were digging endlessly. I hate to think how much dirt we had moved before the neighbor discovered what we were doing. Of course, Paul's parents ordered us to fill in the hole immediately. In retrospect, digging caves did not work out.

Arthur Temple lived several blocks from us. He was the principal owner of Temple Lumber Company, and one of the most successful businessmen in our area. He was the only man I knew who ran a large business. As I walked to school during World War II, Mr. Temple would pick me up in his Cadillac. After a number of rides, it became obvious to me that he was very lonely for his son, Arthur Temple, Jr., who was serving in the war. I believe he was picking me up just to visit with a young person. Nobody could have been kinder or more generous to me than Mr. Temple. It was obvious to him after a few visits that I was really interested in business and wanted to know all about his business. He taught me a great deal as we rode together along Olive Street. I will be forever indebted to him for being kind and caring enough to talk business with a thirteen-year-old boy.

The Temples had been more richly blessed than anyone else in Texarkana in terms of financial success, but Mrs. Temple had polio. She was a lovely, wonderful lady who spent much of her time helping others, and she was determined to overcome this crippling disease. She walked several miles a day, even though she was limping. I watched her go past our house with a severe limp but with a determined spirit. Winter, summer, or anytime, she was determined to conquer this disease. She was, and always will be, an inspiration to me that people must not let adversity get them down.

Years later, my teenage son, Ross, was skiing and broke his leg. He was also competing for the third time to be the world-champion horseman in his age group. The broken leg required him to compete with a full leg cast and quite a bit of pain. Without flinching, he rode through the entire season. He won the championship for the third time—proof that adversity breeds strength—proof that people can overcome disability. I thought about Mrs. Temple that night.

When Ross was a little boy and hurt himself, I would rush over and say, "Ross, are you hurt?"

He would look up at me and say, "Yes, but I am too tough to care."

This was at an age when most of his friends would have been crying. I realized then that I had a special little guy.

We had another neighbor, Dr. Charles Smith, who had been severely injured and who walked with a pronounced limp. He had overcome this adversity to become a doctor with a very successful career. He also was an inspiration to me. As I watched Mrs. Temple and Dr. Smith, I realized how lucky I was that I had no problems that prevented me from doing what I wanted to do.

The Kitchens family lived a block away from us. Dr. and Mrs. Kitchens had two daughters, Elizabeth and Julia. They were my close friends, and we played together a lot as younger children. The great benefit I gained from visiting with the Kitchens was that all of them were so smart and talented. They had received virtually every gift. Mrs. Kitchens was instrumental in tapping the full potential of her two daughters and, for that matter, helping to develop the full potential of all the children in the neighborhood. Dr. Kitchens was a wonderful man who would also pick me up as I walked to school. I have many happy memories of my visits with him.

I began delivering newspapers when I was twelve years old. My first paper route was on the Arkansas side of the city. It was a morning route in a middle-class neighborhood, and it was a great learning experience.

My second paper route was an afternoon route in downtown Texarkana. It was a particularly interesting experience because I was delivering papers to banks, to people who had offices in the bank buildings, and to store owners on Broad Street. I would then work my way to the west end of Texarkana where I delivered newspapers to Father O'Brien and to most of the black lawyers and doctors.

The next time I tried to get a paper route, there were none available. The *Texarkana Gazette* told me that they had two areas where no one delivered newspapers, New Town and Avondale—the poorest black area and the poorest white area in Texarkana.

The circulation manager told me that if I would start a morning paper route in those areas, they would give me a special rate. Newspapers sold for twenty-five cents a week, and the newspaper got seventeen and a half cents a week. If I would build a route in those areas, they would pay me seventeen and a half cents a week and the newspaper would take only seven and a half cents a week. The circulation manager made it very clear that this was a high risk and that it probably would not work.

Consider this situation for a moment. I was fourteen years old, and I was being asked to create a paper route that would take me into the two poorest neighborhoods in Texarkana at 4:30 in the morning. You would not think of allowing your child to go into neighborhoods like that today. At that time, there was no concern at all about my personal safety. The world has changed. We have got to change it back.

I clearly remember going door-to-door and asking if they would like to take the paper. I was amazed that virtually everybody wanted the newspaper. This was particularly interesting when many of the poorest members of our society could not read. I later learned that newspapers were often used as wallpaper and insulation. In the winter, the pages were placed between bedsheets for additional warmth.

All of the streets on my route were sand, not even gravel. I could not ride a bicycle through this neighborhood because the weight of the newspapers would make it impossible to pedal through the sand.

I had my horse, Bee, and realized that this would be a unique and ideal way to deliver the newspapers. Once I had created the route, I would get up every morning at 4:00 A.M., saddle Bee, and ride about two and a half miles to Chance Moore's gas station, where the papers were distributed. I would sit on the curb, fold the newspapers, pack them into newspaper bags, and put the bags across the saddle horn. While I was folding papers, I would visit with my good friend, Buddy McDonald, who worked at the gas station early in the morning.

To get to Avondale, I first had to ride through a middle-class neighborhood known as Beverly. Then I would enter Avondale—a dramatically different neighborhood. I would deliver papers through Avondale, and ride onto Robinson Road to Summerhill Road, and then over to New Town. When I completed the route in New Town, I would ride home. Everything always went smoothly, and I was usually home by 7:00 A.M.

I had great concerns about collecting for the newspapers because these people were so poor. I was surprised that I was getting almost 100 percent payment. The people who could not be at home on Saturday because of their work would leave their quarters in their mailboxes. They were absolutely punctual about paying.

I became good friends with my customers. Again and again, as I rode my horse through these very poor areas, I would think of things I had been taught as a child, and the phrase that came to my mind a thousand times was, "There, but by the grace of God, go I." I felt extremely fortunate to have my wonderful parents and the life they provided me. Delivering this paper route was one of the great experiences of my life because the people on these routes were so kind and good.

Once the newspaper route became successful, the circulation manager became very concerned because I was making several times as much as the typical paperboy, who earned about five dollars a week. He wanted to reverse the rate to the same rate that everyone else was paid.

Again, luck played a role in my life. Several days earlier, I happened to be in the newspaper offices during the lunch hour. The owner of the *Texarkana Gazette*, Mr. C. E. Palmer, had accidentally locked himself in his office and was pounding on the door. I opened the door and let Mr. Palmer out. He asked my name and thanked me.

I thought the actions being taken by the circulation manager were wrong, so I went to see Mr. Palmer. He immediately recognized me, smiled, and thanked me again.

I explained to him that I had started this route with the understanding that I would be paid seventeen and a half cents a week for each paper I delivered, because everybody thought the route could not be successful. I pointed out that I had to ride a horse because the streets were sand, and I had the expense of feeding and keeping the horse shod. He heard me out, smiled, patted me on the shoulder, and said, "We will honor the commitment we made to you." This was a time in Texas when a verbal agreement was better than a written contract is today. Mr. Palmer taught me a business

lesson that I have tried to practice throughout my life—
honor your commitments.

During the summer, my father developed a serious kidney
problem that could only be treated in Shreveport, Louisiana. I
tried to get someone else to deliver the papers because I
wanted to be in Shreveport with him. Nobody else would do it.

Shortly before we had to go to Shreveport, I went from
door to door on the paper route explaining to my customers
that I had to leave to be with my father who was going to have
a serious medical procedure performed in Shreveport. I told
them there would be several days when I could not deliver
the paper, but I hoped they would continue to take the paper
when I came back.

They said, "Son, save all the papers and deliver them to us
when you get back."

I responded, "But why would you want old papers?"

They replied, "Son, if your dad has a serious medical problem, you need the money, so save the papers and bring them to
us when you come back."

That memory will remain with me for the rest of my life.

In addition to delivering newspapers, I also cut grass during
the spring and summer months. Of course, I did not have a
power mower, and it was hot, hard work pushing my mower
through the thick Texas grass. But it was another way to make
a little money.

While I was in junior high and high school, I collected for
classified ads in the *Texarkana Gazette*. The cost for running a
classified ad for three days was $1.50. In some cases, I would
ride my bicycle for eight or ten miles to knock on the door of a
person who had not paid for the ad. Typically, the people had
not sold the product they were advertising and could not
afford to pay for the ad. When a boy, covered with sweat,
knocked on their door and asked them if they could pay for
the ad, in almost 100 percent of these cases, they did. It was

obvious that these were good people who felt obligated to pay their bills. They epitomized de Tocqueville's words, "America is great because her people are good."

The cotton business deteriorated during the war. Dad went to work at the cotton compress as a bookkeeper. My mother went to work as a secretary. My dad missed being in business for himself, and it really bothered him that my mother had to work. Bette and I missed her.

When my dad was able to go back into the cotton brokerage business, I helped him build his cotton office. He decided to relocate next to the cotton compress. Today it might not look like more than a shack, but he and I had fun building it. It means a great deal to me to have been able to help him build it. I was thrilled the day he moved in and was back in business. I have a picture of his office next to my desk.

One of my most vivid memories of building that office was installing the roof. Driving nails while sitting on corrugated tin in the summertime has the effect of branding you on the backside. I was glad when that job was finished.

My dad let me sit in his office and watch as he bought and sold cotton. This was a wonderful learning experience. Although some of the cotton brokers would try to take advantage of the farmers by offering low prices for their cotton, my father always paid them a fair price. I remember asking him why he paid the farmers more. He replied, "Son, these people work hard from April through September to raise this cotton. I just buy it and sell it. They should be paid a full, fair price. In addition, if I pay them a fair price, they will come back year after year to sell their cotton to me. It is good business."

I cannot adequately convey how much the business experience I had with my father meant to me. Today as I sit here in my office, I look over at a picture of Dad in his office that I have kept all these years. The most poignant thing I see is his general ledger hanging from a nail on the wall. Only in America would that man's son have the opportunity to build a worldwide network of computer systems, communicating by satellite, processing financial data for major companies across the world. That is the story of America.

In 1944, Paul Young and I decided that we needed a car. Believe it or not, the state of Texas issued driver's licenses to fourteen-year-olds. We both had licenses. My dad still had his 1929 Dodge he had kept through World War II and until 1947. This probably explains why I sometimes drive cars for eight to ten years before trading them in.

Paul and I shopped around and we found a Model T Ford for twenty-four dollars. It was not in very good shape, but it was a good price. We had a lot of fun with it, but it developed an engine problem. We had to overhaul the engine, but we did not know how to do it. Carl Hill, a black mechanic, had a shop just a few blocks from Texarkana High School. He was my father's friend and he worked on the 1929 Dodge. My dad asked Carl if he would teach me how to overhaul a Model T engine. Carl said he would.

I worked on the Model T Ford in Carl's shop after school and on Saturdays for several weeks. I had to do everything, but Carl coached me.

Carl let me make all kinds of mistakes. For example, he told me that the first step in overhauling the engine was to remove the oil pan from the engine, which I did. He did not think he would have to tell me to drain the oil out of the pan before I removed it. I crawled out from under the engine covered with oil. Carl smiled and said, "I guess you have learned a lesson there."

With Carl's help, I rebuilt the engine. It was a great engine, and I learned mechanical and engineering skills that were invaluable to me as I went through the Naval Academy. Carl did it simply out of love and affection for my dad and my family.

In 1992, Barbara Walters was doing a program that included my childhood. Carl Hill was standing by for an interview, but Barbara ran out of time and could not visit with him. I wish she could have, because he was such an influential person in my life.

In junior high school, I had to write a paper about what I wanted to be when I grew up. At that time, I wanted to be a doctor. I still have the paper, and I have sent it as a joke to the doctors, including Nobel Prize winners, whose medical research I support. I have also sent it to the medical school whose research I support. They are grateful that I decided to pursue another career, because of my limited talents.

During my teenage years, we could not afford to take vacations. However, my parents wanted me to see as many things as I could and to learn as much as I could. How did we resolve this dilemma?

After working all summer, I would take two or three weeks off and hitchhike across Texas. Typically, my dad would give me twenty dollars for the trip, which was a huge amount back then. He would drive me out to the highway, give me a hug, and I was off on a great adventure. I hitchhiked, in total safety, across Texas, down into Mexico, and back. Nobody was rude to me. Nobody tried to abuse me. I spent an incredible amount of time riding in the back of pickup trucks with dogs and other animals, but I felt absolutely safe.

On other occasions, I hitchhiked through Arkansas and Louisiana with no fear for my personal safety. Today, no caring parent would let a teenage boy hitchhike across the country.

On my trip to Mexico, I ran out of money before I got home. As a matter of fact, I only had about a dollar left when I came back across the border. For the first time in my life, I was truly hungry. I arrived at an all-you-can-eat restaurant in Pittsburg, Texas. For sixty-five cents, I made up for a few missed meals. I believe the owner would have paid me that much to stay out of the restaurant that day.

I was able to hitchhike straight into Texarkana because it was not too far away. At the end of the trip, I understood for the first time in my life what it was like to be truly hungry and unable to sleep. With no money in my pocket, there was no place to rest, so I just kept hitchhiking. However, even at 2:00

A.M. on remote two-lane roads, I was absolutely safe. This was a different time in our country's history.

I learned business from my father, my friends, and from experiences I had on my hitchhiking trips. That is why even today, we joke about my being a "roads" scholar.

Today, because I have been so blessed, I have my own airplane. I purchased it secondhand. I bought it at a bargain price, still practicing what my dad taught me when I bought my first used bicycle. Every time I take off I say to myself, "I cannot believe I own an airplane." This is a long way from hitchhiking across Texas.

In 1947, a really big event occurred in our family. My dad bought a new car—a Plymouth—to replace the 1929 Dodge that had wooden spoke wheels. His friends would kid him that he had the only car in Texarkana that had termites. He drove this Plymouth until his death in 1955, and my mother drove it for several years after that.

CHAPTER FOUR
College and the Navy

In high school, I was focused on working and learning to be a businessman. I was not preoccupied with being an honor student, and yet all of my friends—Paul Young, Richard Russell, Bill Wright, Jim Morriss, John Carnahan, and others—were honor students.

A turning point in my life occurred one day in high school when a great English teacher named Mrs. Duck asked me to stay after class. She looked me squarely in the eye and said, "Ross, why aren't you smart like your friends?"

My response was, "Mrs. Duck, I am as smart as they are, but they study all the time. I have other interests."

She said, "Ross, talk is cheap. If you are as smart as they are, let me see some results."

I took the challenge, and I studied night and day. On the next report card, I had all A's but one. For the rest of the time that I was in high school, I had excellent grades. Mrs. Duck gave me the incentive to create an academic record that allowed me to get an appointment to the Naval Academy. She changed my life.

A few years later at the end of my freshman year at the Naval Academy, I had excellent grades in English. I felt a strong obligation to thank Mrs. Duck, so when I arrived in Texarkana that summer, I went to her home and thanked her.

She expressed genuine surprise that I could do that well. This was consistent with the way she had always motivated me.

She then said, "Ross, why didn't you just write me a letter?"

I replied, "Mrs. Duck, every paper I ever turned in to you came back circled with red notes about how I could make it better. I knew I could not write a letter that did not have mistakes in it, and I thought I would be better off to personally thank you."

Without laughing or smiling, she said, "Ross, you are probably right." She kept the pressure on. I owe her a debt I can never repay.

I was an average mathematics student until I met Mr. Forester. He motivated me to study mathematics more seriously. Again, that made it possible for me to get an appointment to the Naval Academy.

His wife was my civics teacher. Mrs. Forester did a brilliant job teaching us about the history of our country and our obligations as citizens. Many of my thoughts and feelings today spring from the experiences I had in her classroom.

After high school, I attended Texarkana Junior College for two years while I was trying to get an appointment to the Naval Academy. Again, I had incredible teachers. Mr. Burrus taught me chemistry and physics. Mr. Glass taught me advanced mathematics courses. Mr. Willis taught my first, and only, accounting course.

Of all the professors and teachers who have influenced my life, Mr. Pinkerton had the greatest impact. When I was President of the Student Council, he was our faculty supervisor. He also taught speech.

I had a number of interesting experiences at Texarkana Junior College. When I arrived, they did not have a yearbook. I felt we should have one, so I led the effort to create a yearbook. This was a great adventure because I had never been responsible for publishing a yearbook, but we got it done.

We also organized an intramural sports system that was a lot of fun.

At the end of my freshman year, I was elected President of the Student Council for my sophomore year.

Mr. Pinkerton taught me to stand on principle, and I owe him a debt that I can never repay. While I was President of the Student Council, the school board that oversaw the college decided to build a new campus on one square block of land across the street from the old college. The old college had a capacity for 200 students. The new college would also have a limited capacity. The students felt very strongly that the campus should be moved so that it could be expanded over the years to serve more students. In a very respectful way, and without protest, we took our ideas to the board, to the Mayor, and to all the community leaders in Texarkana. It was revolutionary for students to express their views, even in a respectful way. Mr. Pinkerton quietly urged me to do what I felt was right.

Shortly after I arrived at the Naval Academy, I read these words on a plaque—"When principle is involved, be deaf to expediency." Commodore Maury spoke these words in 1849. I immediately thought of Mr. Pinkerton. He taught me that.

I took a pretty good beating for having spoken out, but in the end the college was moved to the larger campus because it was the right thing to do. Today, this is a college where a student can get a four-year education without leaving his hometown, and 5,100 students are enrolled. Mr. Pinkerton gave me the courage to stay the course. I learned a great deal from him. One of the buildings on the new campus is named in his honor.

The Dean of Texarkana College was another wonderful man, Dean W. P. Akin. He was a great educator who was personally involved with every student.

During this time, I continued my efforts to get into the Naval Academy. My family did not have any political contacts, and all we could do was write letters to Congressmen and Senators. During my sophomore year at Texarkana College, out of the blue, I received a telegram from Senator W. Lee O'Daniel, offering me an appointment to the U.S. Naval Academy. Of course, I was thrilled. This had been my dream. Josh Morriss, Jr., the son of the owner of Offenhauser Insurance, the sponsor of our Boy Scout troop, had gone to the Naval Academy. He had been one of my role models as a child.

My friends in Texarkana could not understand why I wanted to go to the Naval Academy. I had never seen the ocean, I had never seen a ship, but I knew that I wanted to go to the Naval Academy.

Josh Morriss, Jr. had told me about his experiences at the Naval Academy. Of course, I was not nearly as talented as Josh. Prior to the Naval Academy, he had gone to MIT. MIT would not have accepted me.

Bill Harkness and Hugh Longino had also shared their experiences at the Naval Academy, and that was enough for me.

I graduated from junior college in June of 1949 and was scheduled to go to the Naval Academy later that month for my physical to determine whether or not I would be accepted.

Dr. N. B. Daniel was our family doctor. He and my father were close friends. Their offices had been next to each other on the second floor of the Beck Building in downtown Texarkana, until we built my dad's new office next to the cotton compress.

Dr. Daniel gave me a thorough physical before I left for the Naval Academy. He was confident that I would pass the Navy physical.

Our neighbor and good friend Dr. A. W. Roberts, an ophthalmologist, examined my vision. He thought that I could probably pass the Navy eye test, which required 20/20 vision, but told me that it would be a close call. Dr. Roberts advised me to rest my eyes for several days before the exam. I followed his advice.

I took my first commercial airplane ride at the age of nineteen to go to the Naval Academy. I left Texarkana on June 20,

1949, on American Airlines Flight 402 at 10:42 A.M. The ticket cost $75.61. The plane was a DC-3. I was the first person in our family to fly on a commercial airliner. The plane made several stops before arriving in Washington, D.C.

When I arrived in Washington, D.C., I took a Greyhound bus to Annapolis. I stayed in the same home that Josh Morriss, Jr. had stayed in when he entered the Academy. It was owned by Miss Jennie Collinson at 1200 West Street.

It took several days to take the physical. Everything went fine until they started studying my nose. I had a badly broken nose. The doctors said that I would have to go home to get it operated on. In addition, I had one tooth that needed filling, and the doctors said I would have to have it filled before I could be admitted.

Miss Jennie helped me find a local dentist, who repaired the tooth.

Captain Reed, who headed the medical unit at the Naval Academy, said, "Son, you are going to have to go home and have your nose operated on."

I said, "Captain, I cannot."

He asked, "Why not?"

I said, "I cannot afford to."

He asked, "How did you break your nose?"

I explained to him that it had happened while breaking horses.

Luck was with me, because he was a horse lover.

He broke out laughing and said, "We will admit you to the Naval Academy, and we will operate on your nose while you are here."

They never operated on my nose, so it is still the same twisted nose that I had when I entered the Naval Academy, but thanks to Captain Reed's kindness and generosity, I was accepted. Again, luck played a huge role in my life.

One of the most talented people I knew growing up was a boy named Mitchell Young. He had all the gifts—great leader, great athlete, great scholar. He was an outstanding football player, at the top of his class academically, extremely popular, and he had a great personality. Mitchell received an appointment to West Point. He was older than I, so I watched him very carefully because I hoped to go to Annapolis someday. Mitchell had seriously cut his hand as a boy, and that wound caused him to fail the physical at West Point. The day that I passed the physical at the Naval Academy, I spent a lot of time thinking about the fact that Captain Reed had let me in even though my nose was broken, yet Mitchell Young, who was far more talented than I could ever be, had not been able to get into West Point because he had cut his hand at an earlier time. Luck plays a big role in your life. Mitchell Young went on to become a very successful doctor, with a wonderful family. He still lives in Texarkana. Every time I look at his hand, I think about how fortunate I was to pass that exam.

Many years later, I met Don Ephlin, the Union Leader at General Motors, when I was on the General Motors Board of Directors. Don was so talented as a young man that he was accepted at MIT, but he could not afford to go. He was accepted at West Point because of his talent, but he failed the eye exam. There is not much that you can do about your eyes. They had to be 20/20 to get into a Service Academy. Fortunately, I passed the eye exam.

Don Ephlin spent his life on the factory floor. I had a world of opportunities opened to me because I was able to go to the Naval Academy. Don Ephlin's story has a happy ending. After retiring from General Motors, he lectured at MIT, the school he could not afford to attend as a young man.

At the time, I wondered how I finally received an appointment to the Naval Academy, but I never asked. Years later, after EDS was successful, a man who had been an aide to Senator O'Daniel called me and said, "Ross, didn't you ever wonder how you got an appointment to the Naval Academy?"

I responded, "Yes, but I was not going to ask."

He said, "I was cleaning up the senator's office one day and said, 'Senator, we have an unfilled appointment to the Naval Academy.' The senator asked, 'Does anybody want it?' I said, 'Well, there is this boy from Texarkana who has been trying to get it for three years.' The senator said, 'Give it to him.'"

He said, "Ross, your name never came up."

I concluded then, as I have all through my life, that luck plays a huge role in a person's life, and this will explain why I have said repeatedly that I am probably the luckiest man alive in this country today—first because of my parents, and second because of this opportunity and the many others that I will discuss later, including Margot, my five wonderful children, and the great adventure I had in building a successful business. I have had more than my share of great luck.

I was sworn into the Naval Academy on my nineteenth birthday, June 27, 1949.

When I entered the Naval Academy, I was surprised that they issued me several pairs of shoes. I had never had more than one pair of shoes at a time, and I could not understand why they would give me so many pairs of shoes at once. This was possibly my first example of government waste.

Later, I learned that the different types of uniforms required different colors of shoes. I also learned that we were expected to have perfectly shined shoes at all times, so I needed two pair, just in case one pair was scuffed. The Navy issued a dozen sets of underwear. I had never had more than three or four sets of underwear in my life.

At the Naval Academy, I was initially worried that I would not react well to being confined. In Texarkana, I had a great deal of freedom. At the Naval Academy, I was going to be locked up from June through December. As it turned out, there was so much to do inside the Naval Academy that I never felt restricted.

Plebes were paid three dollars per month. I saved my money, and I always had spare cash. I was heeding my father's advice—"Nobody ever went broke with money in the bank." My classmates could never understand how I saved money.

The best part of my first year at the Naval Academy was meeting and getting to know outstanding young men from all forty-eight states (this was before Alaska and Hawaii were admitted to the Union).

The Navy assigned roommates during the first summer, a period known as plebe summer. I was unusually fortunate to have a fine young man named Lyle Armel assigned as my roommate. We became best friends, and we remained best friends until his death a few years ago.

Lyle was from Lawrence, Kansas. His father was in public relations at the University of Kansas. Lyle's dad served in the Navy in World War II and achieved the rank of Captain. Unfortunately, Lyle's father died before Lyle was admitted to the Naval Academy.

Lyle's mother was a saint. She lived in Washington, D.C., and would visit us on weekends. She would always bring great cookies, cakes, and other treats that we were allowed to keep in our rooms.

At the end of the summer, plebes were allowed to select their roommates. Lyle and I were roommates for four years.

The day I met Lyle, I noticed the beautiful picture of his girlfriend, Barbara Lee Rhodes. I met her and realized that she was not only beautiful, but she was also a wonderful, talented person with a great personality and sense of humor. I was best man at Lyle and Barbara Lee's wedding immediately following our graduation. Lyle was best man when Margot and I married. After graduation, we were assigned to different ships, but we kept in touch and visited whenever we could. Margot and Barbara Lee became good friends.

Lyle had a distinguished career in the Navy. He commanded several ships, fought in Vietnam on the river patrol where he was exposed to Agent Orange, and was the aide to

Admiral Arleigh Burke when he was in charge of the Atlantic Destroyer Fleet.

Lyle and Barbara Lee had three children, Tom, Lyle, and Martha. Tom is a career Navy officer. Lyle is a career Marine officer. Martha is happily married with children.

Lyle died of cancer, possibly as a result of his exposure to Agent Orange in Vietnam. I had the privilege of visiting with him on many occasions during his illness. He did not want radical treatment that might prolong his life a few months. Instead, he and Barbara Lee took a trip to Australia and had a wonderful adventure. He died a few months later.

During my last visit with Lyle, he reminded me that we had lost friends, years ago, who were killed in Vietnam.

Lyle said: "Ross, I am very lucky. I got to come home and be with Barbara Lee and our children while they were growing up."

I have had a lot of great friends, but I will have only one friend like Lyle Armel. Barbara Lee and I stay in close contact. We miss him.

I was surrounded by gifted people at the Naval Academy and learned a great deal from them. Jerry Weinstein worked closely with me as our class secretary. Carl Trost was Brigade Commander and went on to become Chief of Naval Operations. Dick Dean was one class behind me and served as President of his class. He later became Brigade Commander, served in the Marines, and achieved the rank of General. It was quite a privilege for a boy from Texarkana to be associated with such outstanding people.

Two other close friends of mine were Bill Leftwich from Memphis, Tennessee, and Bill Lawrence from Nashville, Tennessee. Rarely does God give one person all the gifts. Both of these men were great scholars, great athletes, great leaders, and role models to other midshipmen at the Naval Academy.

Bill Lawrence became a naval aviator. He served as Aide to the Chairman of the Joint Chiefs of Staff. He flew in combat in

Vietnam, where he was shot down by a missile and captured. He served six terrible years in prison in Hanoi, returned home, and became an Admiral. He was Superintendent of the Naval Academy and Chief of Naval Personnel. He is now retired and lives in Annapolis, Maryland.

Bill Leftwich, my classmate from Memphis, came from a prominent family. He did not have to serve in the armed forces. He did not even have to work, but he wanted to serve his country, and when he graduated, he volunteered to join the U.S. Marine Corps. He served his first tour in Vietnam and received every honor a man can receive except the Medal of Honor. It was generally believed that if he had been in any branch of the service other than the Marine Corps, he would have been awarded the Medal of Honor, but the Marines have extremely stringent requirements for that medal.

When he returned from Vietnam, Bill was chosen as Aide to Assistant Secretary of the Navy John Warner. When he completed his tour, Secretary Warner told him: "Bill, you can have any assignment you want. What do you want to do?"

Bill said, "I want to go back to Vietnam."

The night before he left, Bob Hope was hosting a huge dinner at the Waldorf Astoria. He had invited Margot and me to attend. We arranged for Bill and his great wife, Jane, to go with us. We had a wonderful evening. After dinner, we went to their room. Bill put on his uniform and went back to Vietnam. That was the last time I saw him.

Several months later, at three o'clock in the morning, Secretary John Warner called me; his voice was cracking with emotion.

These were his words: "Ross, we have lost Bill."

I could not believe it. Bill did not have to go back to Vietnam. He chose to go back to Vietnam. He was leading a recon battalion composed of many recon teams. He had a policy that anytime a recon team got in trouble, he would personally lead the rescue. Bill rescued the recon team, and as the helicopter lifted off, the blade hit the edge of a cliff. The helicopter fell to the ground and Bill was killed.

Bob Bell was one of Bill's close friends and his roommate at the Naval Academy. He later became an Admiral. Neither Bob nor I will forget our trip to Memphis to Bill's funeral. As I stood there and watched Bill's two little boys and his wonderful wife, Jane, standing in front of his casket, my heart broke.

I prayed that those two little boys could each grow up to be the kind of man their dad was. Thanks to Jane, they did. Bill, Jr. graduated from Virginia Military Institute and served as an officer in the Marine Corps. His brother, Scott, graduated from the Naval Academy and served as a Pilot in the Navy. They have now retired. I know that Bill is looking down from heaven, smiling and very pleased. They are two chips off the old block.

The first year, plebe year, was challenging but interesting. At the end of the year, all of us were evaluated for the first time in terms of our leadership skills. We were evaluated by our classmates, the upperclassmen, the military officers, and the academic officers. The results were posted on a bulletin board. I was shocked to learn that I was ranked at the top of the class in leadership. It was like learning that I could play the piano by ear. I had never realized that I had any special leadership skills.

I continued to be ranked at the top of the class in leadership in each of the evaluations. These evaluations took place three times a year during my sophomore, junior, and senior years. Obviously, my mother and father had been wonderful teachers. My parents' teaching me to "treat other people the way you would like to be treated" was a valuable lesson.

During our plebe year, one of the upperclassmen was very difficult to work with. He would barge into our room and ask if we had any food. Both Lyle's mother and my mother were constantly sending us cookies and fudge. The upperclassman really liked chocolate chip cookies. He would eat the entire supply every time we had them. Lyle and I decided that we needed to put a stop to this, so we had a friend bake a large number of chocolate chip cookies, but substituted Ex-Lax for the chocolate chips.

The upperclassman found them right away and started eating them. Of course, he developed a severe case of diarrhea. His solution was to eat more cookies. This went on until he emptied the box. He finally figured out that the cookies had caused his problem. We never told him what was in the cookies, but he never came back looking for food after that experience.

At the end of our first year, my classmates elected me to be Vice President of our class during our sophomore year. I was also elected President of my class during my junior and senior years.

During my senior year, I was also chosen to be Chairman of the Honor Committee. The Superintendent, Admiral Joy, asked me to rewrite the Honor Code. This was an interesting and challenging experience.

The President of the United States, Dwight Eisenhower, visited the Naval Academy one Sunday. To my surprise, the Superintendent asked me to escort the President on a tour through the Naval Academy. It was a great privilege for a boy from Texarkana to escort President and Mrs. Eisenhower. I will never forget it. No Secret Service agents accompanied us. Times have changed.

During my senior year, one of my good friends, Eugene Johnson, kept urging me to meet a girl named Margot Birmingham, who was a good friend of the girl he was dating. His girlfriend, Mary Lou Off, had met me, and felt that Margot and I would be a good match.

I was hesitant to agree to this blind date because Margot was a Yankee from Pennsylvania.

Margot was hesitant to agree to this blind date because she was not particularly interested in meeting a Texan.

We finally agreed, and on October 18, 1952, we met for dinner on a Saturday night at the Ann Arundel restaurant near the Naval Academy. I was very much impressed, and we had a great evening.

Margot returned to Goucher College. All of her friends who had heard the conversations about dating a Texan rushed up to her and said, "What is he like?" They love to tell this story.

Margot hesitated for a brief period and said, "Well, he is really clean looking."

Margot really hates that story, but I love it. We dated as often as we could during my senior year, and the rest is history.

An interesting coincidence occurred on our first date. Ruby Neil Hart was Milledge Hart's mother, and the wife of a Texas farmer and cattle raiser, Milledge Hart, Sr., with whom my dad worked. Mr. Hart died when his son Milledge, Jr. was a small boy. Ruby Neil became the postmistress in New Boston and raised her son alone. He received an appointment to the Naval Academy and went on to become a Marine officer and later an outstanding businessman.

Ruby Neil was visiting Milledge at the Naval Academy the weekend that I met Margot, and one of my most treasured possessions is a picture of Milledge, Margot, and me standing in front of Bancroft Hall, taken by Ruby Neil. When she returned home, she gave my mother a very positive report about Margot, even though Margot was a Yankee.

On my first cruise as a midshipman, we went to Jamaica, Rhode Island, and New York City. I was asked to clean one of the boilers as we were coming down the East Coast to New York City. I was inside the boiler for approximately fourteen hours. The sailors told me to come outside to see the Statue of Liberty. We were at the foot of Manhattan Island when I walked above deck. I have a photograph of myself covered with soot, looking at the Statue of Liberty.

This was also my first view of Wall Street. Little did I know . . .

During my senior cruise aboard the USS *Missouri,* I was the Midshipmen Commander. We visited Bergen, Norway, and London, England. While in Bergen, I bought my parents a Norwegian cuckoo clock, which we still have today. In London, I bought my mother a hand-painted tablecloth, which she treasured and used at every family event for the rest of her life. It is still in our family, and we use it on special occasions.

I was selected as a Naval Academy representative for *Who's Who Among American College Students* during my junior and senior years at the academy. Upon graduation, I was selected by the Superintendent to receive the *Award for Outstanding Leadership.* The military officers also selected me as one of America's Outstanding Student Leaders. I was honored to receive these awards.

My parents and Bette drove all the way from Texas in the 1947 Plymouth for my graduation. I have wonderful pictures of them with Margot and Mother pinning on my officer bars at the conclusion of my graduation ceremony. I was particularly pleased that my dad, who never finished high school, could attend my graduation. Both of my parents made great sacrifices so that I could have this opportunity. Their presence meant a lot more to me than receiving a diploma.

The Naval Academy conducted a lottery to determine assignments for the graduating class. Each person drew a number. I drew number 254 out of 925.

There were four destroyers going around the world! This was an adventure too good to miss for a boy who had grown up hitchhiking through Texas, Arkansas, and Louisiana—particularly one who had studied world geography endlessly in the Texas schools, but had never visited other countries.

I could hardly wait to get on one of those ships. Obviously, everybody wanted those ships. Three of them were listed together, and the fourth one was located in an obscure place on the list. To my great surprise, no one had selected the fourth ship by the time my turn arrived. I picked the fourth ship, the USS *Sigourney*.

After graduation in June of 1953, I spent some time with Margot at her home in Pennsylvania, and a lot of time with my folks in Texarkana. I bought my parents a window air-conditioning unit to provide cool air for their bedroom. Initially, they thought it was a waste of money, but they quickly adapted to it.

At 2:00 A.M. on June 27, my twenty-third birthday, I reported aboard the USS *Sigourney*. At sunrise, we got under way for an incredible adventure—a cruise around the world. It was a dream come true, and I was being paid to be part of it! We were scheduled to cross seventeen seas and oceans and visit twenty-two foreign countries!

The *Sigourney* had a great skipper, great executive officer, and a great crew. The enlisted men were products of the Depression. Most of them were high school graduates. I noticed an interesting similarity among all the crew members—even those who had not graduated from high school. Everyone could write well. Contrast that situation with today, when some college graduates are barely able to write complete sentences.

I was the junior officer onboard. The bad news is that because we were going around the world, there would be no new junior officers on board, so I got all the dirty jobs. For example, I was assigned to shore patrol everywhere we went. This is not necessarily a dirty job, but it is a challenging job.

Also, I was the ship's chaplain. I had no prior experience in conducting religious services. I worked very hard to prepare a service every Sunday on the fantail as we went across the Pacific. The Korean Truce had not been signed, so there was a distinct possibility that we were still going into combat, even though the truce had been agreed upon. The fantail was filled every Sunday. Judging from the size of the crowd I was drawing, I began to think that I might have the skills of Billy Graham.

In addition, one of my jobs was to teach damage control—how to keep the hatches closed and protect the ship from sinking. In times of imminent danger, there is nothing about damage control that a sailor could not be taught in an instant. They were more than eager to know every detail.

After leaving port, we cruised the Atlantic Ocean to the Panama Canal. Even though I had looked forward to seeing the canal for the first time, I was still overwhelmed by the sight. Reading about this engineering feat as a child is one thing, but actually getting to see it is quite another. I stood there, spellbound, watching the locks raise and lower our ship. It was a marvelous experience, and I loved every minute of it.

After we reached the Pacific Ocean, we headed north to San Diego, and then across the Pacific. When we arrived at Wake Island, the Korean Truce had been signed. From that point on, the attendance at the weekly religious service aboard the ship dropped dramatically. I suddenly realized that everybody had been worrying about his ticket to heaven. After the truce was signed, they figured they could stop worrying. It also became much more difficult to teach damage control during peacetime.

We had great adventures going to Hawaii, across the Pacific Islands and on to Japan. Our home base was in Sasebo, Japan, when we were not stationed off the Korean coast.

I could write a book about the experiences I had while on shore patrol with these sailors. They never seemed to miss an opportunity to have a lot of fun. I had to pick them up from some very unusual places and bring them back to the ship. Despite all of the rowdiness, there was one constant—*nobody ever used illegal drugs*. Illegal drugs were readily available in most foreign ports, but every sailor understood that drugs would destroy your mind and body. Nobody touched the stuff.

When we got to Japan, I was amazed at the quality of Japanese craftsmanship. I saw a man sitting on a curb drawing pictures with a pencil from photographs. I took him photographs of Margot, my parents, and Bette. He drew four beautiful pictures, which I still treasure today.

I could not resist buying my mother twelve place settings of Noritake china for ninety dollars. She cherished it, but she immediately gave it to Margot upon our marriage. We keep it in our family and still use it on special occasions.

I had read about Mikimoto pearls, and while I was in Japan, I visited the Mikimoto Pearl store in Tokyo where I bought Margot a pair of pearl earrings.

I also found a beautiful embroidered kimono in Japan that I gave to my mother. She wore it for the rest of her life.

One of my most interesting experiences occurred off the Korean coast. Captain Lienhard received orders to perform a water depth survey on the 38th parallel to make certain we knew the depth of the water. In the event the truce failed, it was possible that all military personnel would have to be quickly evacuated. I was assigned the job of measuring the depth of the water.

Just across the 38th parallel, standing on the beach, were armed North Korean troops. We were sitting off the beach in a wooden boat for a couple of days taking depth soundings. This made us clay pigeons for their target practice had they so decided. The North Koreans did not bother us because they knew we had massive naval firepower on the ship. After two or three days, we completed the project.

When Captain Lienhard reviewed the maps, he named the navigation points for the people who had worked in the boat. There was one area named Point Perot. Captain Lienhard had put us on the map!

We had so many adventures on this cruise. One of my favorite memories—and this says a lot about the Navy, Captain Lienhard, and Commander Stock—was when we arrived in Hong Kong at Christmas. We held a Christmas party for the Chinese orphans. Since I was the junior officer, I had to plan it. This included a tour of our ship. It was wonderful to see the sailors rallying around to make sure these children had a great Christmas.

When we left Korea, we continued our trip around the world through Hong Kong, Singapore, Ceylon, the Suez Canal, across the Mediterranean to Italy, and the French Riviera.

Toward the end of our cruise around the world, we went into Naples, Italy. I found a store that sold Borsalino hats, and I bought one for my dad. Over the years, my dad had mentioned that the greatest cowboy hats in the world were made by Borsalino in Italy. I gave it to him when I came home. He wore it for the rest of his life. I still have it, in its original box, in my closet.

One of the most vivid learning experiences I had on this trip was on the Riviera. I realized that I would see yachts for the first time. I had always read about them and how they were supposed to be the ultimate toys. I went to the yacht basin. These people had the ultimate place to go have fun, and yet they were all sitting around on these multimillion-dollar toys, looking bored.

Then I realized—and I have had this confirmed again and again throughout my life—that tangible things do not bring happiness. Happiness is a state of mind.

That message was drilled into me on the Riviera as I watched the people on their yachts. It was wonderful to see the beautiful boats, but the people did not look like they were having fun. I contrasted this to the times when our family went to the county fair, or to Spring Lake Park in Texarkana for a picnic. We would laugh, play, run around, and have the time of our lives.

We returned to the United States in March 1954. The first thing I did was visit Margot in Baltimore. She was still at Goucher, and it was great to see her again. She was in her junior year. I would drive up to Baltimore on the weekends, whenever I could, and have a date with Margot. Our romance, now two years old, continued to flourish!

When we were in port, I would drive from Norfolk to Baltimore in my 1952 Plymouth every Friday night to visit Margot. Typically, I had three or four enlisted men in the car with me who lived in the Washington-Baltimore area.

One of our more colorful events occurred when we were stopped one night in a small Virginia town for exceeding the speed limit by five miles an hour. We were taken to the home of the local Justice of the Peace. He considered the case and decided that I would have to pay a twenty-dollar fine. I opened my wallet to pay the fine, and he saw a hundred-yen note that was still in my wallet from the trip around the world.

He got all excited and said, "What is that?"

I replied, "Japanese money."

He said, "Son, give me that hundred-yen note, and we will not even make a record of your speeding."

I gave it to him. It was worth thirty cents.

We immediately left the area and laughed all the way to Baltimore; but after that, we always traveled through that town very carefully.

Every time I had a chance, I would go home to see my parents. During my trip around the world, I had written them several times a week about places they could only fantasize about seeing. They kept every letter.

We always had a great time when I got back to Texarkana. My parents really made it clear that they were proud of me. That meant everything in the world to me, because they had sacrificed so much to give me these opportunities. It was wonderful to see them, even though my father's health was deteriorating.

After two years on the USS *Sigourney*, I was transferred to the USS *Leyte*, an aircraft carrier. This was another great adventure. My first job on the aircraft carrier was in gunfire control, and later I was Assistant Navigator.

My father had a heart attack in 1955 while I was aboard the *Leyte*. I rushed home immediately.

Mother was with him all day, and I would spend every night with him in the hospital, sleeping on a cot. I will never forget those days. It was like my boyhood. We were together for hours. We visited with each other and had as much fun as two people could have. One night, after Dad and I had a long visit, he said, "Son, let's turn off the lights and go to sleep."

I slept in the room with him. The next morning, November 21, 1955, when I awoke, he had died in his sleep—a wonderful way to go when your time comes, to die quietly.

I had the burden of driving home to tell my mother face-to-face that the man she adored and devoted her life to had passed away. We went back to the hospital together to say good-bye to the most wonderful husband and father anyone could ever have.

Immediately after the funeral, I took my mother home from the cemetery, put on work clothes, and went back to the cemetery. I had left instructions with the funeral home not to bury my father. I personally buried my father. I did this because it was the last thing I could do for him. It was a direct way for me to express my love and appreciation for all he had done for me. Coincidentally, Henry Phillips, my boyhood friend who broke horses with me, worked for the funeral home. He was at the cemetery and helped me.

On many occasions when I have been with my fifteen grandchildren, I have often thought that if God would grant me one wish, it would be that my father could have lived to know his five grandchildren and they could have known him and have the wonderful experiences of being with him that I had as a boy. We know that he looks down from heaven on them, and I know he is smiling.

It was a very difficult period for my mother after my father passed away, but she was a strong Christian lady, and she just kept marching forward. I took care of her, just as my dad had taken care of his mother. As soon as I got out of the

Navy, Margot and I spent a lot of time with her. She would come to Dallas, and we would go to Texarkana. We were very, very close.

My sister, Bette, became a Girl Scout executive after she graduated from Texas Christian University. She later became a teacher in the Fort Worth school system, and then she became a Vice-Principal in the Fort Worth schools. In 1969, she assumed the responsibility of Director of The Perot Foundation. She was close to Mother and would also travel to Texarkana frequently.

Margot graduated from college in 1955 while I was serving on the USS *Leyte*. She taught school for a year in Baltimore, and I would go to Baltimore to visit her as often as I could. I finally convinced Margot to marry me.

I clearly remember the day that Margot and I shopped for her engagement ring. We bought it in Baltimore at Tyson's Jewelers. It cost eight hundred dollars. That almost cleaned out my bank account, but it was worth every penny. Years later, Ross Jr. gave this ring to his fiancée, Sarah Fullinwider, as her engagement ring. Even though the diamond is tiny, Sarah was pleased because she knew how much our family treasured this ring.

Margot and I married on September 15, 1956. The captain of the USS *Leyte* was also a pilot. To maintain his proficiency rating, he was required to fly several hours each month. Captain Martin was kind enough to fly me from Quonset Point, Rhode Island, to Pittsburgh. Margot picked me up at the airport at Pittsburgh, and we got married in Greensburg, Pennsylvania.

Mother and Bette were there, and that made the day even more special. The only sad thought I had that day was that my dad was not there. Lyle Armel was my best man.

Finally, I had won Margot. The best luck of my lucky life! I met her on a blind date. She was a beautiful girl. I was gone all the time. Every doctor at Johns Hopkins (just to mention one college in Baltimore) wanted to date her. But to make a long story short, somehow I was able to convince her to marry me—"and that's the rest of the story," as Paul Harvey would say.

We had a very modest one-week honeymoon driving along Skyline Drive, eventually arriving in Rhode Island where the *Leyte* was docked. One of my treasured possessions is a picture of the two of us sitting on top of a mountain in that beautiful part of the country. There we were, sitting on top of the world!

We were driving my secondhand 1952 Plymouth from place to place and having a wonderful time. We ate several meals at Howard Johnson's restaurants. Our favorite dish was deep fried clams.

We really splurged and stayed a day or two at The Greenbrier, a beautiful hotel in West Virginia. The room was fifty dollars. That was expensive for us, even though it sounds cheap today.

We moved into a small, one-bedroom apartment in an old wooden house in Wickford, Rhode Island. Coincidentally, it was right across the street from the local Howard Johnson's restaurant. We ate there during the first year while Margot learned to cook. In addition, Margot enjoyed having dinner with me aboard the *Leyte* from time to time.

Margot taught school. I was at sea most of the time, but we treasured every moment we had together.

CHAPTER FIVE
IBM and EDS

One day while I was on the bridge of the aircraft carrier USS *Leyte* working as assistant navigator, Stan Farwell, an IBM executive, a guest of the Secretary of the Navy, and also the brother of our Executive Officer, was watching me carry out my activities. The Captain mentioned to him that I was getting out of the Navy in a few months, and Mr. Farwell came over and said, "Son, would you be interested in a job with IBM?"

I looked at him and said: "Mr. Farwell, I am twenty-six years old. I have worked since I was six years old, and I always had to look for work. You are the first person in my life who has ever offered me a job. You bet I would like to have an interview with your company, IBM, and I do not even know what you do."

He broke out laughing, and said, "You don't know what IBM does?"

I said, "Well, we have IBM typewriters on the ship."

He said, "No, Ross, I am interested in you because the Captain tells me that you have a lot of knowledge about the gunfire control computers, and we are in the computer business."

I said, "It would be an honor to have an interview with IBM."

The rest is history. That is how I got into the computer business. One more time, luck played a huge role in my life. Just by chance, I met an IBM executive. Just by chance, the Captain told him that I was talented in an area where IBM needed people. He was kind enough to offer me an interview. That led to my having a job with IBM and learning the computer business, and that gave me the knowledge and the insight to create EDS.

When I got out of the Navy in June 1957, we packed everything we had in the back of our 1952 Plymouth and drove to Texas. An outstanding gentleman, Henry Wendler, the manager of the IBM office in Dallas, offered me a position with IBM as a sales trainee for five hundred dollars a month. That seems like a very small salary, but I was paid a premium by IBM, because the typical sales trainee at the time was paid four hundred dollars per month. Also, a dollar bought a lot more then than it buys today. Margot got a job teaching at the Greenhill School.

We lived just three blocks from the Highland Park Presbyterian Church, which has been our church home for nearly forty-five years. In all those years, there were just two senior ministers, Dr. William Elliott and Dr. Clayton Bell. They have been outstanding spiritual leaders. My family is grateful, as are thousands of members of this great church.

We enjoyed settling into our first home. We bought secondhand furniture, including a secondhand refrigerator and a secondhand stove. We did not buy anything unless we could pay cash for it. We did not have a washing machine until eight or nine years later. We would go to the washateria to wash our clothes.

We were able to afford a nice, but very small, apartment in University Park at 3660 Asbury, four blocks from Southern Methodist University, in one of the finest and safest neighborhoods in Dallas. The rent for our first apartment was $110 a month, with the understanding that I would cut the grass. A few years ago, the landlord found the contract, framed it, and sent it to us.

We were just as happy the day we arrived in Dallas, with everything we owned in the back of our 1952 Plymouth, as we are today. Happiness has nothing to do with tangible possessions. It has everything to do with your state of mind.

We lived on my salary, and Margot put her salary in the bank. We were following my dad's advice—"Nobody ever went broke with money in the bank."

Margot and I had only one car for several years. In 1959, we traded the 1952 Plymouth in for a 1959 Ford, and in the early 1960s, after Ross and Nancy were born, we bought a Plymouth station wagon so that Margot could have a car.

Working for IBM was one of the great adventures of my life. I had great leaders as managers. Great instructors were teaching me. I had wonderful opportunities with customers, and I happened to be at the right place at the right time in a brand-new industry with the finest company in that industry. IBM is one of the finest companies in the world, thanks to the principles of Tom Watson, Sr. His son, Tom Watson, Jr., carried those principles forward.

IBM reinforced every leadership principle that I had been taught in the Navy. It was a role model of what a company should be. I worked night and day for five years at IBM. I was lucky to have been a part of such an incredible adventure.

Years later, after EDS had become successful, I was skiing at Vail. I walked into a restaurant one day, and someone shouted out, "There is the one who got away." I looked across the room, and there was Tom Watson, Jr. with Senator Percy.

I went over and spoke to Mr. Watson, who had been kind enough to make a sales call with me when I was a salesman. He asked me to sit down and said, "Ross, why didn't we take your idea?"

I reminded him that at the time IBM made the decision, 80 percent of their revenues came from hardware and 20 percent came from software.

He said, "Well, why were you interested in the 20 percent?"

I laughed and said, "Mr. Watson, when you are not getting either part of it, the 20 percent looks good."

We both shared a good laugh and agreed on that point.

He said, "Did you have any idea that the ratios would change dramatically in favor of the software?"

I said: "No, Mr. Watson, that was just pure luck. I had no idea that software would become a bigger factor than hardware in the total cost of producing information."

The last contact I had with Mr. Watson was to receive the Independent Award from Brown University in 1988. Mr. Watson had recommended me for this award, which is given to independent thinkers. This award is in my home. Each time I look at it, I think of Mr. Watson and my great adventure with IBM.

Two Dallas businessmen taught me a great deal while I was working for IBM. One was Bob Bourland, who was an officer of Blue Cross of Texas. The other was Bill Underwood, who was an officer at Southwestern Life. I learned a great deal from both of these men, and I will be forever grateful for their advice and the time they spent with me.

Margot and I were already having the time of our lives. Just when it seemed that things could not get any better, they did. We received one of God's greatest blessings—our first child, Ross, Jr., was born in 1958. Margot and I were ecstatic!

We had been trying to get Mother to move to Fort Worth or Dallas, but she did not want to leave Texarkana. Once she learned that Margot was pregnant and there was going to be a new baby in the family, that did it! She moved to Fort Worth to live with Bette the day Ross, Jr. was born. Over the years, Ross, Jr. and the later grandchildren received a great deal of love and attention from her. She was a major force in shaping the lives of our five children. They loved her—no, they worshipped her. There was no place they would rather be than in Grandmother's house, in Grandmother's arms, with Grandmother entertaining them.

My career with IBM in Dallas was filled with excitement. I was associated with some of the finest people I have ever known in my life. I went through the training program, which included basic training in Dallas. We learned how to wire the

IBM 402 and 407 accounting machines. We also learned how to wire collators and calculators, and we learned how to write programs for the IBM 650 computer. This computer had a drum memory. We learned to program the early IBM 704 and 705 vacuum tube computers.

The 305 RAMAC was the first random access computer that stored large amounts of data that could be retrieved immediately. One of my greatest adventures was installing the first 305 RAMAC delivered in Dallas.

I was busy installing this computer at a motor freight company on November 7, 1958, the day Ross, Jr. was born. I raced home, picked up Margot, and took her to the hospital. After Ross, Jr. was born, I made certain that he and Margot were fine. Then, I had to go back to make certain that the computer was running properly.

Before returning to check on the 305 RAMAC, I went to Neiman Marcus and bought Margot a beautiful string of pearls to celebrate the birth of our first child. Sarah, Ross, Jr.'s wife, wore these pearls at their wedding twenty-six years later.

The random access computer worked. It seems unbelievable now, but that computer only had two hundred program steps of memory. Today a small laptop computer has more memory, but that was in the 1950s, and it was exciting to be part of the early days of this new industry.

I attended the IBM sales training course in Endicott, New York, and was pleasantly surprised when I graduated first in my class. My childhood sales experiences—Christmas cards, flower seeds, newspapers, magazines, bridles, and saddles—had paid off.

The first large transistorized computer was the IBM 7070. Over half the transistors came from Texas Instruments in Dallas. Texans were very proud of that.

I had an opportunity to sell a model 7070 to Southwestern Life Insurance Company. I was fortunate to make that sale. They purchased the 7070 for $1,250,000 rather than leasing it from IBM. This was a big event in IBM. I also had the Blue Cross account in Texas. I sold a 305 RAMAC to Blue Cross.

A lot has been said and written about my sales career. It is important to understand that I was selling computers at a time when companies were buying their first computers. It was like selling umbrellas when it is raining.

Our first daughter, Nancy, was born on July 7, 1960. She was a wonderful addition to our family. Her middle name is Elizabeth, Grandmother Ray's first name. I again went to Neiman Marcus and bought a diamond pin to celebrate the birth of our first daughter. Nancy wore that pin at her wedding.

We bought our first house in 1959. It was located in far north Dallas at 6041 Linden Lane, and had two bedrooms. Ross and Nancy shared a room. The house cost $21,000. This was a big moment in our lives. We had a fenced-in yard, so we immediately bought a golden retriever puppy we named Amber. I remember watching Ross sitting on the back steps talking to Amber. History repeats itself.

People have asked me again and again, "Why did you have more sales than the other salesmen?" The answer is that I had been trained all my life by my dad to work hard.

Also, at IBM, the more you sold, the more you made. This goes back to my boyhood—the more magazines I sold, the more garden seeds I sold, the more newspapers I sold—the more I made. I had always been paid based on what I had produced. Working hard to make better pay was something I had been taught since childhood. The only difference between my work and the other salesmen's work in the Dallas office was that I worked longer hours, and that produced more sales. I was not focused on achieving my quota; I was already meeting my quota in less than eight hours a day. I was focused on giving my customers the best possible service and making as many sales as I could.

IBM became concerned that I was making so much as a salesman that it would be difficult to promote me. They wanted to reduce my territory so that I could not make as many sales.

I went to the IBM manager and said: "I want to stay busy all the time, so please do not cut back my territory. If you want to cut back what I am paid, you can do that, because I agree that you pay me more than I am worth, but you do not pay me much until I make a sale. Please do not cut back on my opportunities to work hard all day, every day."

It never occurred to me that they would actually adopt that approach—letting me keep the big territory, but cutting my commission rate—but they did. The last year I was with IBM, I had the largest quota in the western region and was paid 20 percent of the normal sales commission for each sale I made.

In connection with commissions and quotas, a story has floated around for many years about my meeting the annual sales quota during the first nineteen days of January. The story is true, but some details are missing. I had been working in my sales territory for several years, and I had lined up a number of good prospects. These customers were ready to buy the computers at the beginning of the year. There was no reason to delay these sales, so I turned in the sales orders during January 1962. I also figured that since I was only getting 20 percent of the usual commission, I had better collect it as soon as possible.

I quickly discovered the downside to this strategy. I was underchallenged and frustrated. In the meantime, I had developed what I thought was a really good idea—to sell a fully operational computer system to the customer. Anyone could buy a computer, but many customers could not tap its full potential. The customers wanted a system that worked, which required providing the hardware, the software, the programming, and operations, all at a predetermined price.

IBM, to its credit, took my idea to the top of the organization, but they ultimately rejected the plan. At that time, 80 percent of the revenues in the computer business came from hardware sales, while only 20 percent were derived from software sales. IBM believed they had the hardware market locked up, so they did not anticipate a significant change in the hardware-to-software sales ratio.

I was satisfied that IBM had given my idea full consideration and deliberation.

I was driven to do this. I could not decide whether to try it on my own. I really did not have enough money to try it on my own. One day, while sitting in a barbershop, I was reading an old *Reader's Digest*. I read the observation by Henry David Thoreau, "The mass of men lead lives of quiet desperation."

I said to myself, "That is me; I have got to try my idea."

At the same time, I was receiving letters from the Navy encouraging me to return to active duty. I felt that I had a fallback position to support my family if the business failed.

For reasons that I still do not fully understand, I was just driven to create this new company.

I could not decide the name of this new company. One Sunday, while I was sitting in church, I wrote down some names on the back of a church pledge envelope. I concluded that the best name would be Electronic Data Systems.

On June 27, 1962, my thirty-second birthday, I started Electronic Data Systems, as a one-man organization.

As I sit here writing this book, looking at the picture of my father sitting in the office he and I built, looking at his ledger hanging from a nail on the wall, it is hard to believe that EDS is now a company with over 140,000 employees and annual revenues of $21.5 billion. Only in America could an ordinary person have an opportunity like that.

The first thing I did was go to Southwestern Life. They had purchased a 7070, and I knew they had unused capacity. I worked out a plan with the company to sell this excess time. There were 110 Model 7070 computers installed in the United States. I intuitively believed that some of these users must need additional capacity. Selling this computer time would provide the capital to start hiring systems engineers. Southwestern Life agreed to give me that opportunity.

Blue Cross approached me and asked if I would work on a part-time basis to help them in their computer department. I agreed to do that. Blue Cross understood that I was in the process of building a new company. I was paid eight hundred dollars a month by Blue Cross.

My salary when I left IBM was eight hundred dollars per month. My total compensation was approximately thirty thousand dollars per year with commissions. We had managed to save quite a bit of money, and we had saved all of Margot's salary, so we were very liquid. This goes back to my dad's teaching when I was a child: "Pay cash for everything. Nobody ever went broke with money in the bank."

We had the ability to pursue our dream.

Margot was 100 percent supportive. There was no question in her mind that I could succeed, and there was no fear or trepidation. I was almost ready to start, but there was one more thing I wanted to do. I took Margot to Hawaii. We had a wonderful trip and came back to the mainland on a cruise ship. I remember thinking every day that I was the luckiest man in the world to have Margot and our two children. Flying in airplanes and sailing on a cruise liner was very different from hitchhiking across Texas.

Most of the Model 7070s were installed on the East Coast and the West Coast, with a few concentrated around the Chicago area. I started with the East Coast, moved over to the West Coast, and then I moved on to the Chicago area. After making seventy-seven sales calls, I had not sold a single minute of time on the 7070. The clock was ticking, and I was running out of money.

Then I went to Cedar Rapids, Iowa, where Collins Radio was located. Collins was in desperate need of more 7070 time and immediately began flying planeloads of computer tapes and people to Dallas.

For the next six weeks, we processed data around the clock for Collins Radio. After we had paid our bills, we had a hundred thousand dollars in the bank! We then had the money to begin hiring systems engineers!

I would not have made it through those six weeks without the help of two great young men. Cecil Walters was a skilled 7070 operator. He came in during the evenings after his regular job with the Agriculture Department. Dick Beck was a skilled computer operator with Southwestern Life. After he finished his shift with Southwestern Life, he worked night and day with Cecil and me.

When the project was completed, Collins Radio complimented us on our outstanding staff, service, and support. The facts were that we had no staff, service, or support—just Cecil Walters and Dick Beck. They made the difference. If they had not performed, there would not be a company named Electronic Data Systems today.

I decided that I would have two years' salary in the bank or signed long-term contracts that would guarantee two years' salary for each person I hired. This would allow me to protect the people who joined the company in the event that the company was not successful.

The first person to join EDS was Betty Taylor, an outstanding young lady from Farmersville, Texas, the home of Audie Murphy, our most decorated hero in World War II. There must be something in the water in Farmersville, because Betty Taylor was a hero in building EDS. She carried out all the secretarial and administrative skills, typed and prepared all of the proposals to customers, kept all the books and financial records, and produced the payroll every two weeks, just to mention a few things.

The second person to join us was Tom Marquez. Tom had grown up in Colorado. His parents were really outstanding and totally devoted to their children. His dad was a cattle trader, meaning that he would buy cattle and sell them a very short time later at a higher price. Tom's childhood was similar to mine in that he spent a great deal of time with his dad, learning about business, trading, and negotiating. Tom's parents saw to it that he was an excellent student. In addition, he was a superior athlete and earned an athletic scholarship to Notre Dame University. After graduating from Notre Dame, he entered Southern Methodist University to obtain a master's degree in business.

In order to raise the money to pay his tuition, Tom sold encyclopedias door to door. One day, he happened to make a sales call at the home of Jim Campbell, an executive with IBM in the Dallas office.

Jim's wife, Jane, visited with Tom, heard his presentation and was very impressed with him, but did not buy the books. She told Jim about an outstanding young man who had tried to sell encyclopedias to her. Jim Campbell called Tom and told him he would like to interview him at IBM.

Tom said, "First, I would like to make a presentation to you about why you should buy a set of encyclopedias for your family."

He made the presentation and sold the encyclopedias to Jim. Jim then interviewed Tom, and Tom joined IBM.

I had known Tom as a sales trainee at IBM and had been very impressed with him. He had a lovely, talented wife, Carolyn, who I knew would be very supportive of him and a real asset as we built the company.

At the same time that I was interviewing Tom, I was interviewing Milledge (Mitch) Hart, the son of one of my father's friends from New Boston. I have already talked about Mitch and his mother. As you may recall, both of them met Margot on our first date at the Naval Academy.

Mitch's father died when he was a small boy and his mother did an unbelievably outstanding job of rearing him and helping him achieve his full potential. As we were growing up, I would see him several times a year. Because our mothers were close friends and spoke often over the telephone, I would hear even more frequently about all of his many accomplishments.

Mitch entered the Naval Academy during my senior year. He had a great record at the Academy and went on to become a Marine. He had an outstanding record in the Marine Corps, and when he left the Marine Corps, he joined IBM in Dallas. He had just completed sales training and was in the middle of some projects that would not allow him to join us immediately, but he came aboard a short time later.

Tom and Mitch had the same mission—to sell new customers. When we started, we did not have a single customer. We worked night and day to build a customer base for our new company.

Jim Cole was considered to be one of the most outstanding systems engineers in our part of the country. He could make these new computers do anything and could produce the results that the customers so badly wanted, but in many cases, were unable to achieve. We had worked together on several projects and had become good friends.

Jim had a very secure position and a bright future with IBM, and it was a major decision for him to take the risk of joining a start-up company that, at this point, was just an idea. He decided to join EDS, and this gave us a great start in building our systems engineering team, because when other people saw Jim Cole come aboard, they intuitively felt that this must be a good opportunity.

Tom Walter was one of our first systems engineers and later went on to become the Chief Financial Officer of the company. I met Tom aboard the USS *Sigourney* as a young naval officer. A few months after he reported on board, Admiral Rickover interviewed him for the Navy Nuclear Power Program. Only the top 2 percent of the most intelligent people in the Navy were interviewed by Rickover. Tom was selected and successfully completed the nuclear power program. Normally after completing the course, graduates go to sea aboard submarines, but Tom was kept as an instructor—a tremendous compliment to his engineering skills.

Tom was working for IBM in Atlanta. We contacted him, and he agreed to join EDS in Texas. He was one of the principal reasons that EDS succeeded. We were lucky to get him.

Obviously, I was surrounding myself with people who were far more talented and gifted than I was. This was the secret to EDS's success—the multiplier effect of all this talent.

Tom Marquez called on Mr. Williamson, the Chief Financial Officer of Frito-Lay, one of the most prominent companies in Dallas. One of Mr. Williamson's favorite stories was that when Tom walked into his office, they shook hands and Mr. Williamson asked him, "Who are you with?"

Tom looked back over his shoulder and said, "Mr. Williamson, I am not with anybody. I am all by myself."

He then explained to Mr. Williamson that he was with a new company, EDS, and that we would be in a unique position to help Frito-Lay gain a competitive advantage through its information systems. Mr. Williamson heard him out and was impressed.

We were getting close to making a sale to Frito-Lay when IBM suddenly organized a team to put us out of business. At the time, we were greatly concerned; but in retrospect, this turned out to be a blessing. We knew we had to be at our very best to win, or we would fail.

The IBM team got the senior officers from Republic National Bank and the partner of a major accounting firm that was the CPA firm for Frito-Lay to join them in a meeting. They told Herman Lay, the founder of Frito-Lay, that doing business with us would be a terrible mistake and could ruin Frito-Lay. Mr. Lay, Mr. Williamson, and Mr. Lavorne heard them out.

After they left, Mr. Lay looked at the other Frito-Lay officers, smiled and said: "Isn't it interesting how all these huge companies are reacting against this new company, EDS. These boys must have something special."

Years earlier, when Mr. Lay started his company, he personally cooked and sacked the potato chips and delivered them to his customers. He knew what it was like to start up a new company and was very supportive of EDS. We made the sale to Frito-Lay—EDS's first sale that included a long-term contract. As I recall, its initial monthly revenues were approximately $5,168.

Mitch also worked night and day with the senior officers of a great life insurance company in Dallas named Mercantile Security Life Insurance Company. When the President, Ned King, and the Senior Vice President, Jim Bailey, decided to do business with EDS, they became our second substantial account and long-term contract. This contract produced revenues of about $4,000 per month.

As I recall, these first two contracts were five years in length.

A third company, Continental Emsco, sold oil field equipment. Tom Marquez led the marketing effort for this sale. The company President, R. C. Reeder, and the Comptroller, Bob Blair, were deeply involved in the decision. Once again, we were successful, and the revenues from this contract were approximately $10,000 per month.

With these contracts, we had reached a "critical mass" that allowed the company to grow and make a profit. We continued our sales efforts and were successful in selling Transport Life Insurance Company, Great Commonwealth Life Insurance Company, Independent American Life Insurance Company, and Lane Wood, a mortgage factoring company.

Later, Frito-Lay and Pepsico decided to merge. Mr. Lay arranged for us to have an opportunity to make a presentation to the senior officers of Pepsico. Several months later, we were able to make a very large sale to Pepsico in New York, and this opened up a whole new world of opportunities—thanks to Herman Lay.

Obviously, we needed more systems engineers. Tom Marquez led the recruiting effort to find great engineers and bring them aboard. He was very fortunate to attract two outstanding men, Jim Messerschmitt and Jim Meler to assist in recruiting.

Our problem was that there were not enough great systems engineers. This was a time in the computer industry comparable to the period shortly after the airplane was invented. At that time there was a shortage of pilots who knew how to fly. In our case, we had a shortage of engineers who knew how to make computers produce results for the customer.

The early systems engineers who created EDS's outstanding reputation for quality and service were led by Jim Cole. They included Dick Dean, Tom Downtain, Rusty Gunn, Charlie Miller, Chuck Folsom, Bill Starnes, Bob Watkins, Clair Peters, Ann Ellis, John Tignor, Mike Maurer, Jim Young, Bill Gaylord, Paul Chiapparone, Don Clark, Bruce Bygate, Ed Frantz, Earl Spraker, and Jim Senseman. These great systems engineers delivered results on time, on schedule, and on budget to our customers, which was really unusual in the early '60s computer business. Their performance made it clear that nobody did a better job than EDS.

In the meantime, Cecil Walters, our first computer operator, led the operations effort, and he and the recruiters found great operators, including Dalton Heidelberg, Gene Shipman, Leo Harris, Roy Cole, and Don Dansby. These were the pioneers who always got the job done and created the solid granite foundation to build a great company.

At this point, Betty Taylor had far more responsibilities than any one person could handle, and we agreed that we needed to create an accounting department. My mother had been processing our payroll for several years. She did it flawlessly.

We interviewed a number of accountants and chose an outstanding young woman, Diane Folzenlogen, who did a magnificent job. From the early days, she made our accounting and financial departments as perfect as humanly possible. These departments were a source of great pride to the entire company.

Once we had established our reputation, we were able to sell our services all over the United States. Our principal challenge was finding enough systems engineers to do outstanding work for our customers.

Recruiting continued to produce great engineers, but we finally realized there just were not enough outstanding systems engineers. We decided to start a training program to train young people to become systems engineers and computer operators. This was very controversial inside the company because it took time and was expensive.

We had recruited a really outstanding man, David Behne, to join us as a systems engineer. We asked David to lead the effort to create a training program. He did an outstanding job and within a very short period of time, the training program he created produced skilled systems engineers and computer operators in the numbers we needed, and grew to the point that we were training several thousand systems engineers and computer operators each year.

When the history of EDS is written, David Behne's name should go down as one of the key people who gave EDS the ability to keep growing and achieve its potential during that critical time when there was a shortage of systems engineers and operators.

The first person to join us as a trainee was Bill Starnes, a really outstanding person and Naval Academy graduate. Bill completed the training program and became a legendary systems engineer and builder of EDS.

Our recruiters had to find outstanding people who had the aptitude to become systems engineers, and they searched all across the country looking for them. Our principal source of trainees was young officers returning from thirteen months in combat in Vietnam. We chose them because we felt that they would have excellent leadership skills and a unique degree of maturity, even though most of them were no more than twenty-five years old. In addition, we recruited top graduates from state universities.

We had a thorough screening method to determine which of these people had the aptitude to learn systems engineering and operations, and learned a great deal about how to select people who could be successful. Within a few months, we had dropped most of the conventional thinking about choosing trainees, including a written aptitude test.

These great young people who learned these skills went on to accomplish impossible tasks again and again—on budget, on schedule or ahead of schedule. The result was terrific customer satisfaction. More importantly, as the company grew, they had the leadership skills to lead and motivate the ever-increasing numbers of employees.

During this period, we were only hiring people with prior work experience and young officers who had just returned from Vietnam. The recruiters met a college graduate, Les Alberthal, who was unusually talented. Everyone who interviewed him was impressed, but he did not have several years of work experience or service in Vietnam. We made an exception in his case. The people who wanted to hire Les briefed me. I had met him and was impressed. We hired Les, and he later became the Chairman of the company—a great example of not getting trapped by some recruiting formula.

One day a young pilot, Jeff Heller, who had just returned from Vietnam, was being interviewed. Everybody was really excited about him because of his outstanding record from boyhood through college and in Vietnam. Unfortunately, he did not do well on a one-hour aptitude test created by IBM, which was widely used to determine whether or not a person had the potential to become a systems engineer.

We decided to waive the aptitude test in Jeff's case because he was so special. He went on to become one of the greatest systems engineers in the company. He was also one of our most outstanding leaders. He later became the President of EDS.

The stories of Les and Jeff illustrate the point—do not look for people using a formula or a cookie-cutter mentality.

In this period, when our highest priority was to attract great people, I spent a lot of time with recruiting. Our recruiting motto was, "Eagles Don't Flock, You Have to Find Them One at a Time."

In speeches to the recruiters, I tried to describe clearly the people we were looking for. My comments to the recruiters were:

> When looking for new talent, keep the blinders off. I do not care who you are, where you came from, where you went to school, what race, what sex, or what religion you are.

One of the recruiters interrupted me and said, "Do you care about anything?"

I replied, "Yes, I am interested in what you can do and what you have done lately."

Another one of my favorite sayings describing people we were looking for was:

> Bring me people who are smart, tough, and self-reliant. Bring me people who have a history of success since childhood. Bring me people who love to win!

Again, one of the recruiters in the audience said, "What if we run out of people who love to win?"

I replied, "Then find people who hate to lose, but do not hire someone who is in neutral."

Salesmen always have a tendency to overpromise in order to make a sale. Again and again, I drilled into every person in sales the need not to overcommit. In addition, one of our skilled systems engineers was involved in every marketing effort and had the lead in writing the proposal. The systems engineers were going to have to deliver the product, and this kept the overcommitment problem under control.

Again and again, I would coach the sales team—

"Do not ever sell pie in the sky unless you have the recipe to cook it —and can cook it yourself."

We had a very clearly stated philosophy regarding our customers. Every person in EDS, myself included, was available twenty-four hours a day, seven days a week, to serve our customers. The entire team lived that philosophy.

In addition, we resolved that we would only have one class of employee in EDS—a full partner. Everybody had the same health care benefits and retirement plan. Nobody was kept from a chance to rise to the top of the organization. If the most qualified person was a high school graduate, he or she got the job even though several college graduates might be in contention. Furthermore, raises, bonuses, and stock options were available to every employee. All they had to do was *earn them*! If we had a marginal year and the bonus pool was only partially funded, all bonuses went to the frontline troops. The leaders received no bonuses, because it was our responsibility to assure that the financial goals were achieved.

There were no executive dining rooms. All of us ate in the cafeteria together. I would normally sit at a table by myself. Computer operators and systems engineers, without hesitation, would sit down with me and discuss their ideas about how to make the company better. This was the best part of my day!

All of the other people in leadership positions did the same thing. Most of the good ideas that made EDS successful came from the front-line troops working directly with the customers. Every employee in the company could come to see me. This made everybody in the chain of command extremely sensitive to questions and issues raised by people. If team leaders did not resolve the problems, they knew their team members would be coming to see me. I always loved these visits, and most of the ideas that made EDS the company it is today came from people too young and too inexperienced to have such incredibly good ideas—but they had them and—**WE LISTENED TO THEM**.

In many cases, we let a person who had such an idea organize a small team and attempt to implement it with the full backing of the company. Again and again, they would knock the ball out of the park!

When Mort Meyerson, whose name is now a legend in the computer industry, first joined us as a young man, he bombarded us almost daily with creative ideas and changes that he thought would make the company more successful. Interestingly enough, some of the people in leadership positions got irritated. I was impressed by Mort and his creativity. One of the problems in dealing with creative people is that most of their creative ideas will not work, and you have to listen to nine bad ideas to get the idea that could make history. I always considered this to be fun and part of the process.

In Mort's case, I learned quickly that he had a unique characteristic that most creative people do not have—he had the mental self-discipline to filter out his bad ideas. Early in Mort's career when he would come to me with a new idea, my response would be, "Follow your nose." Two weeks later, he would have made tremendous progress, or he would mention to me that once he had gotten into the idea, he decided it would not work and had dropped it. This made Mort unique and special.

To understand why Mort is so creative, you have to know his parents and his background. Mr. and Mrs. Meyerson created a very interesting and exceptional young man.

Mort became the President of EDS and was its principal builder and leader. He took a great little company and turned it into a great big company!

I have taken the last few pages of this story of my early life to talk about other people—the people who really created EDS.

In fact, I owe it all to other people: my mom and dad who gave me the principles and rules that formed the basis of my life; teachers, classmates, friends, and leaders who shaped my youth; my supportive and loving family; the great people I served with in the Navy and worked with at IBM; and finally, the incredible team who turned EDS from an idea into a successful business.

My own story would have been incomplete if I had not introduced you to these people—the people who made it all possible. They are the principal forces that shaped my life.

With Mother and Bette, 1933

My parents, Lulu May and Gabriel Ross Perot

My father's cotton office that I helped build. The two farmers have just delivered the first bale of the season, which was purchased at a premium.

With my horse, Bee, and my dog Shep—1938

On horseback—approximately 1947

My first view of Wall Street. (I had been cleaning boilers for fourteen hours.) Midshipmen's Cruise—1950

Aboard the USS *Missouri*
on the Midshipmen's
Cruise—1952

Battalion Commander
at the Naval Academy

Receiving the Leadership Award at the Naval Academy in 1953 from Vice Admiral C. Turner Joy, who negotiated the Korean Truce

USNA Senior Yearbook photograph

Being introduced to President Eisenhower by Admiral C. Turner Joy. I was chosen to take President and Mrs. Eisenhower on a tour of the Naval Academy.

Margot and my mother, pinning on my Ensign Boards immediately after USNA graduation

My parents and Bette pose with me immediately after USNA graduation, June 1953.

Aboard the USS *Sigourney* on cruise around the world— 1953

Wedding photo-
graph—1956

With Margot on Skyline Drive on our honeymoon in 1956

With Margot and our children—Ross, Jr., Nancy, and baby Suzanne

With Ross, Jr.—approximately 1960

With Ross, Jr.—approximately 1968

With our youngest
daughter, Katherine

Our children—left to right—Suzanne, Carolyn, Ross, Jr., Katherine, Nancy

Our children—left to right—Suzanne, Katherine, Ross, Nancy, Carolyn

With the early members of the EDS team

With Margot when EDS was listed on New York Stock Exchange

With North Vietnamese POWs in a South Vietnamese POW camp in 1970. I visited the camps because the North Vietnamese had asked me to show the same concern for their men who were prisoners that I had shown for the U.S. POWs.

Visiting refugees in Laos during the Vietnam War

Viewing the Magna Carta, loaned by The Perot Foundation to the National Archives in Washington, D.C. It is on display with the Constitution and the Declaration of Independence.

With Colonel Arthur Simons on our arrival at DFW Airport after the successful completion of the Iranian rescue—1979

Meeting with Mrs. Reagan and General Robbie Risner at a conference
on the subject of illegal drugs

Receiving the Churchill
Award from Prince
Charles—1986

Mrs. Reagan at the
Churchill Award
Dinner—1986

Founders of Perot Systems Corporation, 1988
Back (L-R): Meryl Smith, Ross Reeves, Ross Perot, John King, Gary
Wright, Pat Horner
Front (L-R): DeSoto Jordan, Sally Bell (Administrative Assistant),
Don Drobny
Not Present: Bruce Heath

CHAPTER SIX
Further Biographical Outline

I could write volumes about my adventures with EDS, General Motors, Perot Systems, and subsequent events in my life. The challenges of building a business—from meeting payrolls to building a client base—are both difficult and exciting, but that is another book for another time. Instead of reminiscing about these wonderful experiences, I would rather share with you my thoughts about building a business. You will find these in Book II.

But first, I will include a brief summary in outline form of the major events that have happened since I founded EDS.

- Started EDS in 1962 as a one-man operation.

    Borrowed $1,000 from Margot to start company.

    Company now has 140,000 employees and revenues of $21.5 billion.

    EDS does business throughout the world.

- Sold EDS to General Motors in 1984.

    Served as GM Director and largest individual GM stockholder from 1984 to 1986.

    Sold the remainder of my holdings to GM in 1986.

- Started Perot Systems in 1988.

  After seven years, Perot Systems was twenty-five times larger than EDS when it was seven years old.

  Twelve years after its creation, Perot Systems was as large as EDS was when I sold it to GM in 1984. By the year 2002, Perot Systems was a $1.2 billion a year business.

- Other activities

  In 1968, appointed by the President of the United States as Chairman of the U.S. Naval Academy Board of Visitors.

  In 1969, at the request of the President of the United States, I launched a major project to embarrass the North Vietnamese into changing the treatment received by American prisoners of war. This effort continued until the end of the war in 1973. It was successful.

  In 1979, Col. Arthur Simons directed a successful rescue mission into Iran to recover two EDS employees, Paul Chiapparone and Bill Gaylord, who had been improperly imprisoned. I went into Iran and into the prison where our employees were held. The rescue required the largest prison break in history. The two men were successfully recovered with no casualties.

  Ken Follett wrote a best-selling novel, *On Wings of Eagles*, about the rescue. An NBC TV miniseries was later made about this event.

  My mother was seriously ill with cancer in 1979 when the two EDS employees were taken hostage in Iran. As I prepared to go into Iran, I was concerned that I might not see my mother again. I visited with her in the hospital and explained what we were planning to do. These were her exact words: "These are your men. They did not do anything wrong. The government will not get them out. It is your responsibility to bring them home safely." She knew that we might never see each other again, but that was not discussed. Her only priority was to bring Paul and Bill home.

  The day we arrived in Dallas, she left the hospital and was with my sister, Bette, in a car at the entrance to the airport terminal, waiting to see Paul and Bill greet their families. Mother died a few weeks later on April 3, 1979. This was a very difficult time for our entire family because we loved her so much. As we walked out of the church, my youngest daughter, Katherine, was clinging to me, crying. She looked at me and said, "When I grow up, I am going to be just like Grandmother"—and she is.

After Mother's funeral in Texarkana, Josh Morriss, Jr. approached me about rebuilding the Paramount Theater, where my parents had gone to the movies once a month when I was a child, and naming it in their honor. Bette took responsibility for renovating the theater. The Perot Theater was done to perfection and has been a great source of entertainment and pleasure to the people of Texarkana since that time.

In 1980, served as Chairman of the Texans' War on Drugs committee at the request of the Governor of Texas.

In 1984, served as Chairman of the Select Committee on Public Education at the request of the Governor of Texas.

From 1980 to 1984, served on the President's Foreign Intelligence Advisory Board, a committee to oversee and audit the activities of the intelligence community. Each person serving was required to have the highest security clearances.

In 1984, I purchased the only Magna Carta that was allowed to leave England. This was the Magna Carta that was signed by King Edward I in 1297 and was codified into English law. It is now on exhibit at the National Archives in Washington, DC, next to the Declaration of Independence and the United States Constitution, our documents of freedom.

In 1993, Russia sold many historical artifacts from its space program. I purchased them. They are now on display at the National Air and Space Museum of the Smithsonian Institute in an exhibit called "The Space Race."

- Married forty-six years
- Five outstanding children
- Fifteen perfect grandchildren

In addition to our son, Ross, Jr., Margot and I were blessed with four daughters. They are all wonderful, and I could write an entire book about each of them. While they were growing up, we had nicknames for each of our daughters. Our oldest daughter, Nancy, is "Fabulous Little Nan." Suzanne's are "Special Angel" and "Beautiful Blond Daughter." Carolyn's is "Super Care," and our baby, Katherine, is nicknamed "Top Kat" or "Special K."

My daughters have all of Margot's and my mother's great qualities, and this makes them very special to me.

One of my greatest joys is being with my daughters, my daughter-in-law, Sarah, and their children. They could not be more devoted, warm and loving. They always have the small children in their arms. On several occasions, I have expressed concern that, unless they occasionally put them down, the children will never learn to walk! I know that my mother is looking down from heaven with a big smile. I can sum up my feelings for them with these words, "Thank Heaven for Little Girls!"

I could write volumes about each one of my daughters, but that will have to wait until a later time.

I was concerned that my only son, Ross, Jr., might be intimidated by my success, so I loved him, encouraged him, but left him alone to decide what path he would choose.

Here is Ross, Jr.'s record:

- Three-time world-champion horseman.
- Graduated from Vanderbilt University.
- Completed jump school at Ft. Benning during the summer following his freshman year.
- Completed thirteen-week course in Marine Officer Training at Quantico during the summer following his junior year.
- Learned to fly a helicopter immediately after graduation and became the first person to fly a helicopter around the world, at twenty-three years of age.
- Replaced Charles Lindbergh as the youngest man ever honored by The National Air & Space Museum.

- Received the Langley Medal, FAA Medal, and the Sikorsky Trophy for the helicopter flight.
- Became an Air Force officer, chosen by the other cadets during officer training as the most outstanding cadet.
- Became an Air Force Fighter Pilot.
- Successful businessman and father of four children.

The second proudest moment in my life occurred when an enlisted man nominated Ross, Jr. as one of America's most outstanding young men.

The proudest moment came during a telephone call from Ross, Jr. several months later, informing me that he had been chosen as one of America's Ten Most Outstanding Young Men, when he spoke these words: "Dad, the most important thing to me is that the sergeant who nominated me be present and seated next to you the night I receive the award."

At that moment I knew that my son had his priorities straight.

Today, Ross Jr. is one of the most successful, respected business leaders in Texas.

Ross now serves as the President and Chief Executive Officer of Perot Systems.

He is "Big Ross." I am "Old Ross." I live in my son's shadow, and there is no better place for a father to live.

Ross, and my four sons-in-law—Clay, Patrick, Karl, and Chris—could not be finer fathers. Their families are their highest priority.

Many good things have happened to me in my life, but the greatest reward is to have a wonderful wife, five outstanding children happily married and fifteen perfect grandchildren.

Finally, I will not even start writing about my fifteen grandchildren, because it would require an entire book about each one to explain my love for them.

Years ago, I was asked how it felt to be so successful. I replied, "I will not consider myself successful until my children are grown and are good citizens, with a deep concern for other people and a willingness to translate that concern into action."

Today, my children are grown and are too good to be true, thanks to their wonderful mother.

My five children made a large gift to build a women's and children's hospital. The closing line in their presentation speech says it all—"It is our hope that every child born in this hospital will have a mother just like ours." These words mean more than diamonds or gold to Margot and me.

Book
II
The Principles for Success

The remainder of this book was originally written by me as a gift to my son, upon his graduation from college.

It lists principles that anyone can use. They will guide you no matter what kind of business you are in—or whatever task you have undertaken.

What we are really talking about is how to be a success in life—not just in business. But we will never make any progress in that direction until we can first agree on the answer to the question—

"What is success?"

CHAPTER ONE
What Is Success?

Success is often nothing more than moving from one failure to another with undiminished enthusiasm.
Winston Churchill

Success is doing something you enjoy and doing it well. The teacher, minister, elected official, military officer, or missionary who is the best in his or her field is every bit as successful as the person who makes a great deal of money. The best way to measure success is in terms of personal accomplishment and personal satisfaction.

As a young person planning your career, the most important thing you can do is to be honest with yourself. Nobody else can know you as well as you know yourself. Certainly, no personnel director or recruiter can figure out what you really ought to do as well as you can.

Unfortunately, too many people have stereotyped opinions about what they ought to be or what they ought to become, and they let these override what they really want to be.

• Size yourself up.
• Determine your strengths and weaknesses.
• Plan for a career that centers on your strengths, not your weaknesses.
• Commit yourself to that career.
• Learn how to do it better than anyone else.

Stay Flexible

Probably the most important advice I can give you is to remember that life is not orderly. In many cases, life is not logical. Business and life do not follow the neat lines of an organization chart. Both business and life are far more like cobwebs. As you commit yourself to a business career, remain flexible, realizing that the more you learn about a business, the keener your insight will become about *what you really want to do.*

Do not ever lose the traits you had as a child. As a child, you were totally comfortable in deciding one day to be a teacher; the next, a professional athlete; and without any hesitation, to change to a brain surgeon, plumber, lawyer, jockey, or whatever else suited your fancy. Unfortunately, after you become an adult, you acquire a strong need to be consistent.

Within our company, I occasionally encounter great people who, based on their initial knowledge, selected a position in our business. Over a period of time, they realized they would be better suited in another area of the company. They never discussed it, feeling that the company had invested a great deal of money into training them, and having committed themselves to a job, they felt they should stick with it. The end result is that at some point in time, these people come in terribly unhappy. In most cases, they feel that the company should have intuitively sensed these concerns that they were never willing to discuss with anyone.

We work very hard to keep a climate that allows each team member the personal freedom to choose a different career path, based on additional knowledge and experience.

If you have made a mistake in your career choice, talk to the people in your company. Tell them what you want to do. The more successful you are, the more successful your company becomes. Everybody wins!

The Steps to Success

How does a person become successful?

- Pick an industry that attracts you and something you are on fire to do.
- Choose the company in that industry that has the greatest appeal to you.
- Search until you find a company that you are really excited to join.
- Serve an apprenticeship in that company.
- Learn all about the company and the industry—become an expert.
- Look for unmet needs. Look for markets that are not being served.
- Develop ideas to satisfy those needs.
- Present these ideas to your company.
- If the ideas are sound and your company is sensitive and alert, you will have an opportunity to turn your ideas into reality.

In my case, the company I was working for was not interested in the idea I developed. I decided to start my own business because I was convinced that my idea was sound. That idea is now EDS.

Before you branch out on your own, know yourself. In any large group there are probably no more than two or three people who should start their own businesses. The failure rate of new businesses approaches 100 percent. The failure rate of new businesses started by people who have the capability to start a new business is still extremely high, because of all the pressures and stresses inherent in turning an idea into a successful business.

Pacing Yourself

I have had a unique experience in observing thousands of great people start their business careers. Again and again, I have seen these people approach business as a hundred-yard dash. They initially had great energy, great ambition; but they poured so much energy into their efforts for a brief period of time that they were unable to produce a great sustained performance month after month. Never forget that a business career is a marathon, not a sprint. You must perform consistently over a period of many years.

Nobody has developed a course that successfully teaches people to pace themselves. They have to learn this the hard way—I did.

Probably it is a desirable trait to see this tremendous burst of energy in people starting out in business. Inevitably, they are going to exhaust themselves. Hopefully, they will be tough enough to survive that experience and learn to pace themselves.

Professional or Management Career?

As you build your career, you will have to make another basic decision—whether to develop your career along professional lines or go into management. Unfortunately, in our country many men and women in business today feel that they are failures unless they go into management. My response to those people is—what if Dr. Michael DeBakey, one of the world's foremost heart surgeons, had decided to be a hospital administrator? The world would have lost a gifted heart surgeon.

Our business is the operation of huge computer centers and systems engineering. What would the future be if our most skilled computer center staff and senior level systems engineers all became managers? Our company would lose its greatness. It takes both the professional and the generalist. Both roles are of equal importance. Do not let yourself get confused on this subject and feel that you must force yourself into management, even though you really want to develop your career along professional lines.

Again, know yourself. Know your strengths and weaknesses. Play to your strengths. That is what every winning team does. That is what every very successful person in business must do.

The Importance of People

Whether you plan to develop your career along professional or management lines, I hope that you will learn something that I am deeply aware of—one person is nothing more than a straw in the wind. The sooner you realize how insignificant you are, the more successful your career will be.

This is an easy concept to grasp when you think of management, but it is more difficult when you think of a professional career. Again, use Dr. DeBakey as an example. He works with a small, highly skilled team of doctors and nurses. Let us assume that one morning only Dr. DeBakey arrived to operate. Nothing would happen. Even that great professional cannot perform without a team.

Once you start to realize your own limitations, it is only natural for you to start surrounding yourself with men and women of greater capability than your own. Then, and only then, will exciting things really start to happen.

As you build your career, you must learn to attract and keep great people as a part of your team. Finding and attracting these people is difficult. Keeping them as part of your team is the key to your future. How do you do this?

By creating an environment where their goals and dreams can also materialize.

You must do a number of things to build this environment. It is fragile. Everyone must work very hard to keep it as the company grows. There can be no seniority system. The best-qualified person gets the top job. Constantly work to prevent company politics. Select men and women who wish to build their careers based on what they produce and who would not stoop to building their careers at the expense of others.

Deal with each person as an individual. There is only one class of employee. Do not tolerate one person looking down on another. Discourage an atmosphere where one person would look up to another as a more important person, because that stifles free, open communication. Instead, maintain an environment where each person deals with every other person as a full partner.

Recognize and reward excellence. Who are the top producers? In every possible way, recognize them for their unique contributions.

The Most Successful People

As a result of my business success, I have had the opportunity to meet and get to know the men and women you would consider among the most successful business people in the world today. I think you would be interested in knowing some of their characteristics.

First, there are no geniuses in this group. In terms of mental capacity, they would probably be ranked slightly above average. One characteristic stands out. These people are honest. They do what they say they will do. This causes other people to trust them. This creates an opportunity for these people to lead. Never forget, trust is fragile. It takes years to earn. It can be lost in an instant. It must be re-earned each time you have contact with a person.

Another characteristic of these successful people is that they have a great deal of self-discipline. They are able to stick to the task at hand. They realize that the more successful they become, the more unpleasant the tasks will be that they have to perform.

As an example, our company has a brilliant team of men and women. All of the routine problems, even the tough ones, are handled by them. When a problem gets to my desk, it has repeatedly defied solution. One of the "rewards" for building a successful business, staffed with a great team, is the opportunity to spend most of your time working on the toughest problems facing the business. The most successful men and women have the self-discipline and perseverance it takes to do this and do it well.

Toughness or resilience is probably the most dominant characteristic I have observed in this group. These are people who have the ability to lock onto a problem and pursue it through many disappointments and failures to a successful solution. On occasion, I have felt that the dominant characteristic of these people was that they could not recognize when they had failed, and consequently, they refused to quit, and went on to succeed. Again and again, you will find their brilliant business careers are built squarely on the rubble of their early failures. They turned their early failures into learning experiences.

As a group, these people take a tremendous amount of pride in what they are doing.

Watching them in action is fascinating. They know more about their particular industry than anyone else. As you watch them make decisions in machine-gun fashion, you would conclude that they are making intuitive decisions rather than carefully thought out, logical decisions. In fact, these people are bringing the sum of their total prior experience to bear on a given problem. Their early successes, failures, and disappointments are all focused on the problem at hand. The knowledge they have gained from their past experiences gives them the ability to decide quickly and accurately.

As a group, these people are extremely competitive. **THEY LOVE TO FINISH FIRST**.

Success and Money

The best way to make money is not to have money as your primary goal. Again and again, I have seen great people come into the business world, primarily motivated to make money. Almost without exception, they failed. They missed the real essence of learning to do something well, of building something better than anyone else, and were constantly reaching with only one objective in mind—to make money.

Fortunately, because you live in this country, if you learn to do something better than anyone else, you will find that financial success comes as a by-product. This has been certainly true in my case to a unique degree. Making money has never been one of my goals. I can clearly remember how surprised I was in 1968 when I suddenly realized what a great job the entire team had done in building a company that could generously reward the people who created it and who continued to build it. If we had set out to create a vehicle to make money, I do not believe we would have been successful at all. Instead, we set out to build a great company made up of great people. The financial rewards came as a by-product.

Do not expect the financial rewards to come quickly or easily. You would probably consider me to be quite successful at an early age. It took me fifteen years to build an income that substantially exceeded our family's monthly needs. Unrealistic expectations can damage your effectiveness and potential.

Financial Success and Happiness Are Not Related

In any group, there must be at least a few people who have major personal or family problems, are unhappy for one reason or another, and are saying to themselves, "If I could just make a lot of money, I would eliminate all of these problems and be happy."

I wish there were some way that I could duplicate the experiences that I have had, so that each person starting into business could share these same experiences, compressed into a much shorter period of time.

I can clearly remember August of 1957, when Margot and I drove into Dallas with everything we owned in the trunk of our car. We have been very fortunate since that time. I can honestly report to you, however, that we are not one bit happier as a result of financial success. The births of our five children brought us far more additional happiness than any of the unique experiences we have had as a result of business success.

Based on my experiences and observations of others, I have concluded that if a couple has problems when their income is modest and later achieves financial success, the success only compounds their problems instead of eliminating them. Success causes the marriage to break apart, because with success come many complications, placing additional stress on an already faulty relationship.

If you question what I am saying, I can prove my point simply by suggesting that you walk through a very expensive resort, catering to people who are wealthy. Look at their faces. Watch them. How many of them are having as much fun as you and your family? After my first visit to such a place, I concluded from my observations that happiness and financial success are unrelated.

Avoid Debt

Learning to manage your own money is an important step to success. The people I have met who have been extremely successful made it a point to save money in their early years, when their incomes were small. They avoided the temptation, so prevalent today, of engaging in deficit spending. They realized the need to be financially sound, and resisted the temptation to spend everything they made, or spend more than they made.

Over a period of time, they were in a financial position to make prudent investments and take advantage of opportunities that came their way. Contrast their position with the young couple who is deeply in debt and, in effect, running on a treadmill just to make the payments.

Granted, we live in an age of rising expectations, but as I said earlier, the acquisition of tangible things does not bring happiness. Spending beyond your means can put you under severe and unnecessary stress. I strongly urge you to stay solvent, save your money, plan for the things you want, work for them, wait for them, and when you can really afford them, buy them. Of course, buying a home is an obvious exception, but, again, do not make a down payment on a house you really cannot afford. If you do, you will not enjoy living in it.

Self-Discipline

I mentioned self-discipline earlier. As you become more and more successful in your career, you will need another type of self-discipline. Something in human nature causes us to lose interest in the things we do best, at our moment of greatest accomplishment.

Perhaps the easiest examples to look at are the professional boxers. Starting out, the young fighter knows that he must undergo the drudgery of roadwork and training to keep his body in peak condition. Over a period of years, he wins a series of fights and becomes champion of the world. His name, accomplishments, and boxing skills are spread across the newspapers, radio, and TV stations of the land. He is at the top of his profession.

Something in human nature causes him to start slacking off at this point. He begins to believe his press notices. He thinks he is invulnerable. He eases off on the training and roadwork, and the predictable happens—he loses his crown to some other fighter on the way up.

There is a plaque hanging in my office that sums it up—

"One is never more on trial than in a moment of excessive good fortune."

As you become successful, you will need a great deal of self-discipline not to lose your sense of balance, humility, or the keen assessment of your strengths and weaknesses that you made years ago. Do not let yourself become a dilettante. Study the great corporations in this country. You will see that a common characteristic of these companies is that the people who created them had the self-discipline to stay with them and to continue building them over a period of many, many years.

The old saying "Cobbler, stick to your last"—that is, keep to your own work—is very true in business. Learn something. Do it well. Stick with it. Avoid distractions. Keep your life simple. Never forget who you really are, and most important, never lose sight of those things you cannot do.

To build a successful career, you have got to expect to be involved. You are out on the field—not in the stands.

Theodore Roosevelt summed it all up with these words:

It is not the critic who counts, not the man who points out how the strong man stumbled, or where the doer of deeds could have done them better. The credit belongs to the man who is actually in the arena; whose face is marred by dust and sweat and blood; who strives valiantly; who errs and comes short again and again; who knows the great enthusiasms, the great devotions; who spends himself in a worthy cause; who, at the best, knows in the end the triumph of high achievement, and who, at the worst, if he fails, at least fails while daring greatly.

*The world wants results
—not excuses!*

This is a picture of my father in his cotton office that I helped him build.

Please notice his ledger hanging from a nail on the wall.

Only in America, would this man's son have the opportunity to build a company with a worldwide network of computers, processing financial data by satellite for major corporations.

> These principles for success were written by my father, Gabriel Ross Perot, and given to me as business advice when I was a boy, to help me succeed in my boyhood jobs.

1. The world wants things done, not excuses. One thing well done is worth a million good excuses.

2. Meet obstacles or meet failure.

3. Diamonds are chunks of coal that stuck to their job.

4. A champion is a fellow who gets licked two or three times every week but is still able to call himself a champion.

5. The one who shows up best is the one who shows off least.

6. Luck is what happens when preparation meets opportunity.

7. Your services will not command a premium if your word has to be discounted.

8. It may be farther around the corner of a square deal but the road is better.

9. We must give up many of our small ambitions if we hope to achieve a really great one.

10. Everybody who is doing anything in the world has his troubles.

11. No man's opinion is entirely worthless. Even a ten-cent watch tells the right time twice a day.

12. He who puts all he has into his work usually succeeds because he has little competition.

13. When you have a fight with your conscience and get licked, you win.

14. A clock-watcher never becomes a man of the hour.

15. A fool can tear down a castle, but it takes a wise man to build a log cabin.

16. You cannot dream yourself into character; you must hammer and forge yourself one.

17. A hard fall should mean a high bounce if one is made of the right material.

18. A loafer must feel funny when a holiday comes along.

19. No matter how small your lot in life, there is room enough on it for a service station.

20. The trouble is, we spend too much time thinking about what is going to happen, and too little time making things happen.

21. If you listen thoughtfully, you can learn a lot about a person by noting what he says about others.

22. The man who does not need a boss is usually the man who is selected to be one.

23. Go ahead and do it—it is easier to succeed than to explain why you did not.

24. Faultfinders do not improve the world; they only make it seem worse than it really is.

25. If you must make mistakes, it will be more to your credit to make a new one each time.

26. You do not have to go to the back door if you have something worth delivering.

27. Very few are able to carry a chair while climbing the ladder to success.

28. Use what talents you possess; the woods would be very silent if no birds sang there but those which sang the best.

29. If you can see some good in everybody, nearly everybody will see some good in you.

30. Do what you have to do and do it now—spell now backwards and you have the answer.

31. Minds are like parachutes; they function only when they are open.

32. School is your big job now; are you earning your pay?

33. If you are not afraid to face the music, you may one day lead the band.

34. If you are not afraid of failure, failure will be afraid of you.

35. Those who obey the road signs of experience are the first to arrive.

36. The less you leave to chance, the better chance you have.

CHAPTER TWO

Your Business Career

Every good and excellent thing stands moment by moment on the razor's edge of danger and must be fought for.

- A career in business can be a lifetime adventure.

  It should be pursued with the same positive spirit one brings to an athletic contest.

  Success requires preparation, endurance, and the ability to:

  > Absorb failures without becoming discouraged.

  > Achieve success without losing your sense of who you are and what you stand for.

- Business should be a major part of your life, but not your whole life.

  Do not let it take priority over your family.

  No matter how much business success you have, you will consider yourself a failure if your children do not turn out to be good, successful citizens.

  Never miss your children's activities. Keep first things first.

  Business is not that important.

- Making money should not be your goal.

  Building a great company, developing the world's finest products, and creating jobs for thousands of people are worthwhile goals.

  Making a lot of money is not.

  ### Conduct your business in the center of the field of ethical behavior, not along the sidelines.

  ### Never ask—Is it legal or illegal?

  ### Ask—Is it right or wrong?

- Success in business depends to a large degree on timing and luck.

  Accept this fact and prepare yourself.

- Find something you are driven to do.

  You should be on fire with excitement and enthusiasm to seize the opportunity.

  Follow your instincts.

  They are the sum of your life's experiences.

  Serve an apprenticeship.

  Learn the business.

  Look for niches.

- Be ready to react when an opportunity presents itself.

  Pursue your opportunities vigorously.

  Recognize that you will have less capital and fewer people than your mature competitors.

Use brains, wits, and creativity as substitutes for money and you will have a clear advantage over your wealthy competitors.

- Have a clear, concise statement of what kind of company you are going to build.

The statement should say:

This is who we are.

This is what we are going to be.

Make sure everybody has a copy and clearly understands the goals and objectives and the thinking behind them.

Live them.

Review them periodically.

Update them.

- Be available twenty-four hours a day, seven days a week, to serve your customers.

Make decisions.

Take action.

Never forget that heaven and earth were created in just six days! It does not take forever to do great things!

Go anywhere, anytime.

- You will succeed as a result of developing a great team of people.

Recognize how insignificant you are.

Surround yourself with people more talented than yourself.

Clearly recognize your weaknesses.

Bring strong people into these areas.

Play to your strengths.

Treat every person in your company as an important partner and team member.

The only chance to make the best products is to have the best people.

Allow only A+ performers at every level of your company.

- Avoid perks that separate people.

    Never have an executive dining room.

    Go to the cafeteria.

    Stand in line, eat with the people who have direct, daily contact with your customers.

    Do this for three reasons—

    > Over lunch, you will learn a lot about what is really happening.

    > It's fun.

    > If you eat in the cafeteria, the food will always be good.

    Never use terms like management and labor, white-collar and blue-collar, or executives and workers. Everybody, including you, should be a worker. In fact, you must be the hardest worker in the company.

- If you want to find out how the people feel about their unit leader, take an unannounced tour.

    Walk behind the unit leader.

    Watch people's faces when they first look at their leader.

    > If they grin and say, "Hello, Charlie," that is a great sign.

    > If they smile and say nothing, be concerned.

    > If they look up and look back down, you have a problem.

If they will not even look at the leader, you have got a mess.

- Avoid making business decisions based on stories other people tell you.

    You must listen to the customers yourself.

    Spend a great deal of time personally making sure that you are doing a great job for them.

    Listen to the people in your company who work directly with your customers.

    If the people in your company trust you, they will tell you what the problems are and how to solve them.

- Do not try to grow too quickly.

    Be careful and surefooted each step of the way.

    Reorganize to support your growth.

    Do not let things fall apart and then reorganize.

    Do it early.

    Never forget that you become vulnerable with success. Adversity builds strength. Success breeds arrogance and complacency.

- Relish competition.

    The more brutal the better.

    The bigger the better.

    Always compete to win on every evaluation point.

    If there are seven criteria, win 7-0, and pray that your competitors have a 4-3 mind-set.

    In this case, break your team into seven units—each with a mission to win their points.

    Use small, high-talent teams and hope that your competitors will have huge bureaucratic teams.

Fully tap the creative abilities, brains, and wits of your team.

You will be the underdog—but that also is an advantage.

- Develop a winning strategy, and keep it dynamic.

    Keep changing your strategy as you learn.

    Pray that your competitor has a four-inch-thick strategy book, approved by corporate headquarters, and spends all of his time referring to it, instead of thinking creatively.

    Constantly improve your company.

- Although it is human nature to resist change—

    Be restless.

    Never be satisfied.

    World records are made to be broken.

    Get up every day resolving to make things better.

    Invest profits into new, improved products.

- Thousands of people will depend on you for their jobs.

    You can make a huge contribution to your country. You can create new taxpayers who can afford to buy homes and send their children to college.

- Persevere—The common characteristic of the most successful people I know is their inability to recognize failure. "The same blow that shatters glass hardens steel."

    Remember Churchill's words:

"NEVER GIVE IN, NEVER GIVE IN, NEVER, NEVER, NEVER."

CHAPTER THREE
Leadership

The first rule of leadership—treat other people with dignity and respect—the way you would like to be treated. This principle has been validated again and again over the last two thousand years. It is nothing more than a restatement of the Golden Rule—"Do unto others as you would have them do unto you."

- The principles of leadership are timeless because even in a rapidly changing world, human nature remains a constant.
- Consider the principles of the Boy Scouts—practice them and your chances of becoming a successful business leader will improve dramatically.

  A Scout is honest, trustworthy, loyal, friendly, courteous, kind, thrifty, cheerful, brave, reverent, and helps other people at all times.

  A Scout promises to keep himself physically strong, mentally awake, and morally straight.

  The Boy Scout motto is, "Be Prepared!"

- Consider the leadership principles of Attila the Hun, who was born at the beginning of the fifth century—(from

Leadership Secrets of Attila the Hun, by Wess Roberts, New York: Warner Books, 1985).

By their own actions, not their words, do leaders establish the morale, integrity, and sense of justice of their subordinate commanders. They cannot say one thing and do another.

Leaders must establish a high spirit of mutual trust among subordinates and with their peers and superiors.

Leaders must attach value to high standards of performance and have no tolerance for the uncommitted.

Leaders must expect continual improvement in their subordinates based on new knowledge and experiences.

Leaders must encourage creativity, freedom of action, and innovation among their subordinates, so long as these efforts are consistent with the goals of the tribe or nation.

Leaders must provide direction to their Huns, never letting them wander aimlessly.

Chieftains should never misuse power. Such action causes great friction and leads to rebellion in the tribe or nation.

Chieftains make great personal sacrifice for the good of their Huns.

Chieftains must not favor themselves over their Huns when supplies are short.

Chieftains must encourage healthy competition among their people, but must contain it when such becomes a detriment to tribal or national goals.

Chieftains must understand that the spirit of the law is greater than its letter.

Chieftains must never shed the cloak of honor, morality, and dignity.

Chieftains must hold a profound conviction of duty above all other ambitions.

- Hopefully, I have made the point that the principles of leadership are timeless, because even in a rapidly changing world, human nature remains a constant.

- Always use the word *leadership*—never use the word *management*—when referring to people.

  MANAGE INVENTORIES—**LEAD PEOPLE!**

- You must set the example by being a strong, effective leader who motivates your team to achieve its full potential.

- You must have an atmosphere of mutual trust and respect.

  Employee benefits should be the same at all levels. This gives credibility to the fact that everybody is a full partner.

  Earn trust and respect by treating others as you would like to be treated.

  Trust and respect are fragile. They can be lost in an instant.

- Have an environment where there is no penalty for honest mistakes.

  They are learning experiences.

  They are like skinned knees.

  They are painful, but heal quickly.

  When a member of your team makes an honest mistake, he or she feels terrible.

  Do not chew him or her out.

  Bear-hug them and tell them about your honest mistakes.

  Put it behind them, and get back to constructive work.

  Make sure they understand that you have not lost confidence in them.

  In this environment, people will be open and candid.

- Treat each person as an individual.

  Do not put people into categories.

  Recognize that something inside every human being cries out—

  I am unique.

  I am special.

  There is only one person in the world like me.

  Do not treat me like a commodity.

  Treat me as a human being.

  Treat me with dignity and respect.

- Keep each person challenged to achieve his or her full potential.
- Make your company an exciting place to work.
- Women will make up a significant part of your workforce.

  Make sure you have a company you would be proud to have your daughter work for.

  Have zero tolerance for sexual harassment or vulgarity.

  Personally fire anyone who violates these principles.

Never forget!
United Teams Win!
Divided Teams Lose.

Remember the motto of The Three Musketeers—All for one, one for all!

Every part of your company is equally important.

The people working third shift at entry-level jobs are just as important as the senior officers.

Live this principle.

Give your team strong, intelligent leadership.

Be a person they can trust, rely on, and respect.

- Create an environment where the hopes and dreams of every person can materialize, if the company is successful.

Do not limit stock options to executives.

Make it possible for every employee to earn stock in your company by doing an outstanding job.

Vest these options over five to ten years.

Have an employee stock purchase plan.

This makes everyone an owner of the company.

This causes people to focus long term, not short term.

Everybody will be focused on the target—building a great company.

If most of the people in the company own stock—

You will not have to worry about keeping costs under control.

The entire team will be focused on keeping the company growing.

Measure your success by how many people who work in your company become wealthy.

- Recognize and reward performance.

Listen, listen, listen to the people who do the work.

Personally fire the people who steal, cheat, or take advantage of others.

Create a professional work environment where people are having fun while building the finest products or services.

Recognize outstanding performance the day it occurs with raises, bonuses, and stock options, and thank the great producers publicly. They are your company's heroes.

Have a face-to-face performance evaluation with each person at least every six months.

Tell them—

What they are doing right.

What they are doing wrong.

How they can improve.

Do not keep written records of their evaluations.

Judge people by what they have done lately, not by a mistake they may have made twenty years ago that is still contained in a file.

Get their candid evaluation of the company during each performance evaluation.

Listen.

Take action.

- Ask yourself—

Is it wiser to create an environment where people enjoy their work or hate their work?

Will people be more effective if I treat them as human beings or as commodities?

Am I wiser to have my associates work with me or for me?

Should I listen and act on the ideas from the people who are on the front lines with the customer or ignore them?

The answers are obvious.

- Develop a short course, teaching the principles of leadership. Teach this course to each person assuming their first leadership role, just before they take that job.

Stick to the fundamentals of leadership.

Do not allow administrative matters or filing reports to be a part of this course.

- Become personally involved anytime one of your associates or a family member faces a serious problem.

  Show them by your actions that you really care. If a child of an associate is ill, see that the child receives the same quality of medical attention your child would get.

  Make sure that everyone knows that you are to be notified twenty-four hours a day, seven days a week.

  When the emergency occurs, drop everything and take care of your associate and his or her family.

  Be willing to live on the front lines.

  Eat, live, and fight alongside the troops.

  In hard times, feed the troops first—feed the officers last.

  Do not build a big personal staff.

  Be available to everyone.

  Have a good feel for what is really going on.

- Keep direct contact with customers.
- Never compromise on—

  Integrity.

  The quality of your products.

  Service to your customers.

  The quality of your people.

  The working environment in your company.

- Never be satisfied. Make your company and its products better every day.

CHAPTER FOUR
Making Decisions

- The ability to make good decisions is based on two things:

  Your own knowledge of the subject matter.

  The more you know about a business or subject, the higher the probability that you will make a good decision.

  Your ability to listen to people.

  These individuals will have different technical skills, different business skills, and divergent views.

  You must be able to successfully extract the information from their minds so that you can analyze it and make a well-reasoned decision.

- Will you always make good decisions? No. You are human.

  Your challenge will be to make more good ones than bad ones, and control the losses around the bad ones.

- To achieve this, bring an open and uncluttered mind to each new decision.

  Avoid developing a recipe or cookbook mentality toward making decisions.

  Each situation is unique.

An idea that failed in the past may be successful now because of changed conditions.

Benefit from your past experience, but avoid becoming a victim of it.

- Listen to people whose views are different from your views.

  In many cases, they will be right.

  Your challenge will be to accurately assess their strengths and weaknesses.

  Remember that some of the best thinkers may be the least articulate and have trouble presenting their views.

  Others may present a compelling case, yet propose a bad idea.

- If there are ten factors to be considered, focus on the important ones.

  A common mistake in decision making is to give the same weight to major and minor points.

- Numbers can cause you to make a poor decision. Ask yourself—

  Are these the critical numbers?

  What is included?

  What is left out?

  Are the numbers accurate?

  Do the numbers total correctly?

  Be leery of cash flow numbers and return on investment numbers until you know how these cash flow or return on investment numbers were determined.

  Are the profit numbers pretax or after-tax?

  On large complex projects, find out how firm the numbers are. For example, if building costs are based on an architect's estimate, they will be less accurate than a contractor's bid.

- Go past the excitement of the presentation to the idea itself.
- Do the merits justify pursuing this project?

    What are the risks?

    What are the rewards?

- Look far beyond the risks and rewards presented.

    What long-term obligations do you have to continue paying if the project fails?

    Is this a project that you can stop, or does the very idea put you on a financial roller coaster that you cannot get off of, even if it is a poor business venture?

    If the contract will be in effect for many years, make certain that prices are automatically adjusted to compensate for inflation.

- Do not allow anyone to push you into making a decision.

    Some people are quite skilled at creating—

    Artificial deadlines.

    Imagined crises.

    Illusions of missed opportunities.

    Do not give your approval until you are comfortable that it is a sound idea.

- Avoid undertaking new projects on a grand scale.

    Most ideas can be pilot-tested.

    If the test is a failure, the cost will be quite low compared to a massive project that fails.

- Most bad decisions result from failure to consider factors that later appear obvious.

Your advisors will have developed a box that they believe contains all the variables of the project.

Your job is to mentally go outside the box to look for any additional pitfalls that may exist.

- As a business executive, you will have to make the final decisions.

Get the facts.

Make the decision.

Do not hesitate to alter course later based upon new information.

Never freeze your action plans. Always keep them dynamic.

- Again—be decisive—do not dither around forever.

Problems do not disappear if you avoid facing them. They are like cancer—they keep growing. They get worse!

Follow Churchill's model during World War II—"WE NEED ACTION THIS DAY."

CHAPTER FIVE
Establishing Your Business Reputation

When principle is involved, be deaf to expediency.

- Be honest.

    Keep every commitment you make.

    Never become involved in any business that you feel is immoral or wrong—no matter how much money you think you can make.

- Always be prompt.
- Never take advantage of others.
- Treat everybody as equals.
- Learn your business until you know more about it than anyone else.

    Resolve that your product will be the finest in the world.

    Work harder than anyone else.

- Be the first to step forward when there is work to be done.

    Be willing to undertake the tough, dirty jobs and the jobs involving risk.

    Try to complete each job perfectly.

Take pride in your work.

- Always be courteous, kind, and considerate to those you work with, no matter how busy you may be.
- Pay your bills the day you receive them, especially to small suppliers. They need the money.
- Save money—live within your means.

  Do not buy anything on credit. Save your money until you can pay cash.

  Do not use credit cards.

- Your time is at a premium during the early stages of your career.

  Many activities and people will seek your attention.

    During this time period, it is important that you are learning everything possible about your business.

    Seek out the acknowledged experts in your field and learn all you can from them.

    Do not allow others to control your time with meetings, boards, and civic organizations.

    For several years, concentrate on your business and limit your activity to organizations that interest you.

Live in the center of the field of ethical behavior, asking yourself, "Is it right or wrong?"

Never compromise your principles by running up and down the sidelines wondering, "Is it legal or illegal?"

CHAPTER SIX
Selecting People

***Eagles don't flock. You have to find
them one at a time.***

Your success will be based on your judgment in building a great team of people.

- Build a team of recruiters to go out and find them.

   The people you want will not come to you—you have to search for them.

   Look for people who are smart, tough, and self-reliant.

   Look for people who have a record of achievement since childhood.

   Find people who love to win.

   Such people are self-motivated and will tend to repeat their success patterns.

   Select each member carefully.

   Do not try to "put round pegs in square holes."

   The worst mistake you can make is to look for talent with a cookie-cutter mentality.

   5' 10" tall, blonde, blue eyes, master's degree, etc.

Tell your recruiters to take off the blinders.

Talent comes in all sizes, shapes, races, religions, and both sexes.

Remind them that they are looking for needles in the haystack—very special needles with a small red dot—very special people.

If you find a talented person who has no college education, hire him. You will not be disappointed.

If you run out of people who love to win, look for people who hate to lose!

Stop sales, cease growth—rather than compromise on people.

The team interview is the best filter to select the finest people.

Aptitude tests are not good screening devices.

- Develop a world-class training program to support your growth.

- A common trait of the most successful business people I know is that they were not defeated by failure.

  They learned in the school of hard knocks.

  Their incredible success always included a substantial number of failures.

  The only way to avoid failure is not to take risks!

  Look for people who can withstand adversity. Some people just cannot handle a failure or setback.

  Life and business are full of disappointments.

  Strong people accept these realities and keep going.

- Decide what characteristics the job requires and find the best-qualified person with those characteristics. This may seem elementary, but you would be amazed how often people miss the obvious.

Study a person's leadership background.

>If there is none, and the job requires leading people, the applicant is a poor risk.

Do not hesitate to hire outstanding graduates of state-supported universities.

>They are as bright as the people from the finest private universities in the United States.

>They expect to work hard.

>They do not expect to become a Vice President in one year.

>A good company can earn their loyalty and a career commitment.

- People working in specialized technical areas may get tunnel vision.

  To a large extent, their work may be limited to their specialty.

  Accept this, but look for the people in these specialized areas who have the capacity to grow into generalists and leaders.

  Help them to broaden their capabilities.

- Never forget that God made people imperfect.

  Accept the fact that every person has strengths and weaknesses.

  Play to their strengths.

  No one received all the gifts.

  Accept their limitations.

  Have them work in areas where they are strong.

Do not waste time trying to radically change people.

It generally does not work.

- The smartest people may—

    Be the least practical.

    Have very little common sense.

    Be poor leaders and ineffective in dealing with other people.

    > Leading extremely bright people with these limitations can be challenging because they get frustrated over being so intelligent, yet ineffective in working with others.

- Avoid an applicant with the problems listed below, no matter how talented the individual may be.

    Some people simply cannot tell the truth. They live in a fantasy world.

    Do not have anybody on the payroll who uses drugs.

    People who drink alcohol every day cannot think as well as people who do not.

    > Surround yourself with people whose minds are clear.

    Avoid social climbers.

    Avoid corporate politicians like the plague.

    > These are people who attempt to get ahead at the expense of others instead of advancing based on their own contributions.

- Be careful about hiring recent graduates from the elite colleges, including the top business schools.

    They have been programmed to play corporate games— taking instead of giving.

    They tend to move from company to company.

Their loyalty is to themselves and their futures, not to the company.

Typically, they are fine, outstanding people.

After about five years, they tend to reset their priorities.

At this time, they may be good, long-term prospects.

- Avoid getting close friends involved in your business.

Build a business team that has no history of personal ties.

Base rewards on performance and results.

Be warm and friendly, but keep enough distance so that no one gets the impression that career advancement is based on personal friendship rather than performance.

CHAPTER SEVEN
Marketing

- Even though your company may have the finest products or services in the world—you still have to sell them!
- You must have a world-class sales force.
- Many high-tech companies who have created incredible technologies fall victim to the old proverb: "Build a better mousetrap, and the world will beat a path to your door."

The facts are—

If you build a better mousetrap, you will have to aggressively sell it door-to-door.

As your company grows, it is essential to have a great sales team that can keep a large backlog of orders.

If you fail to do this, your whole organization could be disrupted by a decline in sales.

People could lose their jobs.

The company's reputation could be damaged.

Your personal reputation could be severely damaged.

- Find a world-class sales executive to build your team.

Only consider people who have proven, successful records in your industry as sales team leaders.

Having an outstanding sales record is not enough.

This person must have great leadership and motivational skills to keep the sales team fired up.

This person must be a great leader.

- This sales team will need strong leadership support because salesmen must deal with a great deal of rejection.

Many prospects just say no!

Some say no very rudely.

A great salesman must learn not to take rejection personally and to keep on making sales calls.

One of the keys to successful sales is making a large number of prospecting sales calls each day.

I have personally known salesmen who have become so depressed from rejection that they would not make another sales call on a day when they had been rejected.

At one time in EDS, 80 percent of our customer base had said "no" initially.

The sales force did not give up and later made these sales. Surely this example makes the point.

- The executive you select to build your sales team will then have the enormous task of recruiting the talent needed.

Initially look for a small team of experienced salesmen with successful records in your industry.

You will quickly need to develop a sales training program where you bring in outstanding people and teach them how to sell your product.

This will be a combination of classroom training and tutoring in the field by your most effective salesmen.

The best place in the world to learn to sell is working alongside a skilled salesman in a prospect's office.

- Make sure you have a good system for keeping track of what the salesman does all day.

  The salesman is in the field and may or may not be working hard all day.

  Have a daily reporting system that requires each salesman to account for his or her time during the day.

  Sales leaders must carefully analyze these reports on a daily basis.

  You will find that there is a direct correlation between the number of sales calls and the amount of business sold.

- The sales team leaders should make as many calls as possible with members of the sales force—not sit in the office all day.

- You, as the leader of the company, should make as many calls as possible with your sales force.

  For example, when I was a young salesman with IBM, the President of IBM and the President of the IBM Data Processing Division made sales calls with me.

  They lived in the field.

  They worked personally with the customer.

  They had direct knowledge of what was going on.

- Your sales force should always be compensated based on performance.

  The salesman should be paid a modest base salary.

  Each salesman should be assigned a quota that clearly defines how much is to be sold on a weekly, monthly, and annual basis. This allows performance to be measured at short intervals of time and keeps the sales force focused.

  Make sure your commission plan only rewards the sale of profitable business.

Selling unprofitable business damages your company and damages the morale of people who have to work hard to deliver unprofitable business.

You have an absolute obligation to do a first-class job—even if the project loses money. You must do this to protect your reputation for great quality.

- The commission or incentive plan should be tied to real results and should in no way create an environment where the salesmen could benefit by taking advantage of the customer—or the company.

    The specific details of the sales commission plan will vary widely from company to company and industry to industry.

    It is like a tailor-made suit that must be carefully measured and crafted, but it must also be kept dynamic—continue to improve the sales commission plan as you gain more experience.

    Any sales incentive plan should only reward the salesman for real results that benefit the company and the customer.

    Include in your compensation plan deductions from former commissions for projects that fail to materialize as planned.

- A salesman should not write the contract.

    The contract should be a standard contract, if possible.

    The basic contract and any variations should be approved by someone involved in the production and delivery of the service to the customer.

    This group will be very cautious and conservative because they have to deliver.

Remember, never sell "pie in the sky" unless you have a recipe to cook it!

- Stress, on an almost daily basis, the importance of ethical behavior by your sales force.

  Terminate anyone who violates these principles immediately, no matter how successful his or her sales record may have been.

  This sends a clear signal to the rest of the sales force that you are running a first-class, honest business.

- Whenever a member of your sales force makes a great sale that can have a dramatic, long-term effect on the company:

  Recognize, reward, and honor him or her in front of the entire sales force on the day this occurs, if possible.

  This lets the entire sales force know that the company recognizes, rewards, and publicly honors results.

- As the leader of the company, spend a lot of time in the field listening to the customers directly. Find out directly from the customer how good your sales force is.

- No matter how great your sales force is—

  Keep making it better every day.

  Make it dynamic.

  Always be restless.

  Never be satisfied.

- Finally—

  New business is the lifeblood of your company.

  If sales collapse, your company will fail.

  A great sales force must be one of your highest priorities.

CHAPTER EIGHT
Finance

- A first-class financial team is essential.

  Keep accurate financial records.

    Believe it or not, some people create companies—forget to keep books—and are shocked when they go broke.

- Keep tight control over cash.
- Try to avoid debt.

  Debt is like carrying a boulder on your shoulder.

- Employ a first-rate accountant who—

  Has absolute integrity.

  Is very detail oriented.

  Had excellent grades in college.

  Is both a CPA and has a law degree specializing in tax or corporate law.

  Had experience with major CPA firm.

- Retain a good CPA firm to audit your books each year.
- Make sure your financial records are set up so that it takes more than two people working together to embezzle funds.

For example—

One person approves the bills.

A second person writes the checks.

Another person keeps the books.

Another person reviews the checks.

Personally sign the checks, if possible.

- When you go public—

Make sure stock distribution inside the company is fair.

Only go public if you know you can keep growing.

- Treat stockholders with top priority.

As a major stockholder, cast your fate with the stockholders.

Pay yourself a modest salary. This focuses your financial interests with the stockholders to—

Provide the finest service to your customers.

Keep the company growing.

Keep the profits growing.

Keep the stock value growing.

CHAPTER NINE
Business Partners

Depending upon your business, you may decide to enter into a partnership that will require your continued association with certain individuals over a period of time.

- During the negotiations, if you learn anything about an individual that causes you to question his or her ethics, character, or business judgment, walk away from the deal.

- If you intuitively believe that the individual will not be a good business associate, walk away from the deal no matter how attractive the venture might be.

  Never ignore your instincts regarding other people.

  Following your instincts will keep you out of more trouble than it will get you into.

  Ignore your instincts and a few months later, events will define the reason for the intuitive feelings you had earlier.

- During negotiations to enter into a business venture, if your future partners appear to be dishonest, overreaching, overbearing, unprofessional, arrogant, rude, or caught up in a messy personal life:

  Do not enter into the venture.

Do not waste time negotiating business relationships with people of this type. Either you will not execute the contract, or you will regret it if you do.

- One-time transactions do not pose the same problems as an ongoing relationship.

    For example, in a transaction to purchase a tract of land, you may not even know the seller of the property, but you can complete the transaction by making certain that the contract and related documents have been carefully prepared and reviewed. You will not have to deal with this person after the purchase is completed.

CHAPTER TEN
Business Contracts

- Insist that all business contracts be written in plain English—not legalese.
- Make certain that you and your customers clearly understand and agree on terms, before you commence work.
- On major business transactions, do not let the other side draw the agreement.

    The cost to have the contract prepared is not significant.

    Prepare an outline for your lawyers of the terms you want to include in the contract.

    This approach allows you to control the entire process.

- Identify someone in your organization to read the contract.

    This person should have a keen eye for details.

    Have this person and a lawyer prepare a written outline of the contract in plain English, including all of the escape clauses or limiting factors.

    Read the outline.

    Does it contain every item you wanted?

Then, read the entire contract yourself and make certain that it actually includes these points. Read all of the attachments.

Be aware that one short sentence can contain an escape clause that nullifies pages of guarantees and obligations.

When reading a contract, a person tends to concentrate his attention on the contents of the contract.

Frequently, major items are completely omitted.

Do not limit your analysis to the words in the contract.

- Do not allow salesmen to write contracts.

Prepare a checklist to determine the items that should be included in a standard contract.

Develop a standard contract.

- Allow changes to be made to the contract only through a formal approval process.

CHAPTER ELEVEN
Lawyers

- In my own business career, I have had the good fortune to be associated with outstanding, ethical, principled lawyers.

    In observing other companies, I have learned that lawyers may not be good businessmen. There are exceptions.

- Avoid asking lawyers what you should do.

    Generally speaking, lawyers give advice and options but dislike making recommendations or decisions.

    Tell the lawyer what you want done.

    You are really playing to a lawyer's weakness to ask him to make a business decision.

    You will spend your entire career making decisions, so recognize that you and your lawyer live in two different worlds.

- A bill received from a law firm is a mystery box, much like a child's tangled kite string.

    You cannot unravel it.

    You finally pay it and hope they were honest in accumulating their time.

    Never forget that when you call your lawyer, you will be billed for the conversation. KEEP IT SHORT!

- You will need a good local law firm.

  Recognize the strengths and weaknesses of the firm.

  Be aware that any law firm benefits by developing new skills at your expense in areas of expertise that it does not have.

    Avoid this situation by hiring the best-qualified lawyers in the specialty areas.

- It is probably wise to do business with a number of law firms based on their specialized skills.

  This keeps all the firms on their toes, and will improve the quality of service you receive.

  It will reduce the temptation to overbill.

- As your business grows, you will be able to achieve significant cost savings by developing an internal legal staff.

  Consider hiring a full-time lawyer to work on your staff as soon as possible.

  If you must go to court, you will need a first-class trial lawyer to represent you.

CHAPTER TWELVE
Investments

- With hard work and good luck, you may become wealthy.

  The best investment that you can make is to put the money back into your business.

    The additional capital will enable you to do a better job for your customers and pursue larger customers who require suppliers who are financially strong.

    Even though you may have a large amount of money—never use it as a substitute for the brains, wit, and creativity of your people.

    Money can have a deadening effect on their creativity.

  Resist the temptation to invest outside your business while it is still growing.

    For every good idea you find, you will have to listen to a thousand bad ones.

    It will become a major distraction when your time is best spent focusing on your business.

- If your business enjoys continued success to the point that it seems impossible to reinvest the excess cash, here are a few observations about alternative investments:

  Investing in a business will require your interest and active participation, as well as your capital.

You should not invest in a new venture unless it has a high-talent team capable of turning a great idea into a great company.

Avoid capital-intensive ideas if alternate ideas are available that do not require large amounts of capital.

Recognize that farming and ranching are, at best, money-losing hobbies, unless your "farm" or "ranch" land is directly in the path of development from a major city and that development could mature within ten to fifteen years.

> Location, roads, utilities, schools, etc. are important factors here, but location is the most important factor.

• Spread your risk among different investments.

Do not risk everything on a single venture.

• Understand inflation.

Although it has subsided since the 1980s, there is always the danger that it could return with devastating consequences.

> Make your capital investments in areas that will tend to automatically compensate for inflation.

CHAPTER THIRTEEN
Money

A person is never more on trial than in a moment of excessive good fortune.

- Making a lot of money is more a matter of good luck and timing than genius and planning.
- Be leery of the professional business manager who really believes that he or she can plan it all out.
- Having money is a gift, like the gift of being a brilliant artist or athlete.

   The important thing is what the individual does with this gift.

- Your goal should not be to make a lot of money. If you build a great company—financial success will be a by-product.

   I have lived completely across the economic spectrum.

      Money is overrated.

      It certainly will not buy happiness.

   Money can be a curse—

      It will not bring more happiness to a person and can easily make life so complex that it denies happiness.

      It must be handled very carefully around children.

The ultimate curse is to have children grow up preoccupied with tangible things.

It is important that your children grow up not feeling different or better than others because of their financial status.

- Put your family first!

    Money allows parents—

    To be away from their children too much.

    To have other people teach their children skills they should learn directly from their parents.

    To hire nurses, maids, and other surrogate parents who cannot replace a parent's love, care, and interest.

    Periodically, look at your calendar to determine how many nights each week you are at home with your children giving them your full, undivided attention.

- People can have a great deal of money, yet feel vacant, unfulfilled, and unchallenged. These people miss most of the great adventures of life.

- The great resorts of the world are filled with wealthy travelers who are simply hoboes with money. Walk through these places—look at the faces—notice that hardly anyone is smiling.

- The most important thing is to see that, as your children grow up, they do not become a part of the "idle rich," because this will guarantee an unsuccessful life.

    Do not let your children grow up having the knowledge that you may be setting aside money for them.

    Where is the incentive to excel if they know they will never have to support themselves?

    Observe your friends who grew up with this knowledge.

In many cases, it had a deadening effect on their ambition.

Be careful not to take away the thrill and challenge of creating a place for themselves in life by giving them money.

You cannot give your children too much of your love and time as they grow up. **Your time and love are far more valuable than money**.

- As you pursue your business career, repeatedly ask yourself, "How will I feel about my life in my elderly years?"
- If you do make a great deal of money, remember these words each time you see people in need:

"There, but by the grace of God, go I."

"Help the man who is down today. Give him a lift in his sorrow. Life has a very strange way. No one knows what will happen tomorrow."

- **Give your money generously to help other people. Keep the pledge a child makes in Scouting to "help other people at all times."**

- **Keep your heart filled with love, not hate.**

"He who has a thousand friends has not a friend to spare, but he who has an enemy will find him everywhere."

"Spread the lights of goodness around you."

"It is better to light one candle than to curse the darkness."

"If you will walk toward the light, all the shadows of darkness will fall behind you."

"All the darkness in the world cannot shut out the light of one little candle."

CHAPTER FOURTEEN
Conclusion

If, at the end of your life, you look back and—

You are filled with pride and happiness as you think about your family, and specifically as you think about your children and their qualities;

You have the sense that your business career has been a great adventure;

You have a million happy memories about the wonderful people you were associated with;

Your conscience tells you that you treated each person in your company fairly and generously rewarded them for their outstanding performance;

Your company's great reputation is an enormous source of pride to you; and you did a better job for your customers than anyone else,

THEN, YOU HAVE HAD A SUCCESSFUL BUSINESS CAREER.

You have probably noticed that I did not include making a lot of money. If you keep your priorities straight and accomplish all the goals mentioned above, financial success will occur as a by-product.

I have shared these words with you because it is so important to realize that true success can never come from unethical, immoral, cutthroat methods—the kind of obsessive drive for "success" that seduces some people into believing that anything goes.

Honesty, integrity, square-dealing, compassion—these principles lead to success.

Ultimately, the only things that really matter are God, country, family, friends, and caring for those in need. I can wish you no more success in life than that you enjoy each to the fullest.

APPENDIX
Awards

I consider myself fortunate that I can look back with pleasure at the happy memories of my family and friends and
coworkers who have helped me build businesses of which we
can be proud.

I hope that when people think of me, they recall deeds and
principles that are truly important.

Although neither I nor anyone representing me has ever
sought awards or recognition, I have been honored to receive
forty-seven major awards, along with thirteen honorary doc-
torates. Many of these awards speak of these very issues, and I
would like to share a few of the citations with you.

- Public Service Awards

  Winston Churchill Award – Third recipient; first businessman to
  receive award, 1986

  The Jefferson Award for Public Service – Presented by the American Institute for Public Service, 1986

  Raoul Wallenberg Award – First recipient, 1987

  George Washington Award – Freedom Foundation, 1980

  Theodore Roosevelt Award – Presented by the International
  Platform Association, 1993

  Dwight D. Eisenhower Distinguished Service Medal – VFW, 1981

  Patrick Henry Award – First recipient, 1990

Department of Defense Medal for Distinguished Public Service – 1974

American Legion National Commander's Award – 1970

The Defense Industry Award of the American Defense Preparedness Association – 1986

Peace Through Vigilance Award – Presented by the Marine Corps Reserve Officers Association, 1986

Congressional Medal of Honor Society Award – 1990

Admiral Arleigh Burke Leadership Award – Navy League of the United States, 1990

Military Chaplains National Citizenship Award – 1974

U.S. Special Operations Command Medal – 1995

Air Force Sergeants Americanism Award – 1988

Simons Special Forces Award – 1990

Distinguished Eagle Scout Award – 1970

Lions Club American of the Year Award – 1971

Medal of Honor For Work Regarding Prisoners of War in Vietnam – Presented by the Texas Legislature, 1971

Drug Enforcement Agency Award – 1982

Texas Rangers Hall of Fame Award – 1981

Marine Corps Iron Mike Award – 1970

Outstanding Philanthropist Award – Presented by the National Society of Fundraising Executives, 1986

Award For Courage – New York Boy Scout Council, 1990

Dallas Father of the Year Award – 1984

Outstanding American Award – Presented by the Los Angeles Philanthropic Foundation, 1988

Spirit of America Award – Presented by the Institute for the Study of American Wars, 1989

Spirit of Volunteerism Award – Presented by the Institute of Association Management Companies, 1989

Philadelphia Freedom Medal – 1987

National Urban Coalition Award – 1991

- Business Awards

    Horatio Alger Award – 1972

    National Business Hall of Fame Award – 1988

    Smithsonian Computerworld Award for contributions to the computer industry – First recipient, 1980

    David Sarnoff Award for contributions to the electronics industry – Presented by the Armed Forces Communications & Electronics Association, 1984

    American Academy of Achievement Golden Plate Award – 1970

    International Distinguished Entrepreneur Award – University of Manitoba, 1988

    Man Of The Year In Science & Technology Award – Presented by the Achievement Rewards for College Scientists Foundation, 1986

    Leonardo da Vinci Engineering Award – Presented by the University of South Florida, 1989

    International Computer and Communications World Leadership Award – 1991

    Quarterback of Industry Award – Presented by The Quarterback Club of Washington, D.C., 1986

    Texas Business Hall of Fame – 1986

    American Electronic Association Medal of Achievement – 1986

    Independent Award – Brown University, 1988

    Distinguished Leadership in Business Award – Columbia University, 1991

    Distinguished Leadership Award – Arizona State University, 1986

    Texas Science Hall of Fame, 2001

- Education Awards

    Received thirteen honorary doctorates from universities.

The Winston Churchill Award
February 18, 1986

In recognition of your extraordinary accomplishments in the world of business, the product of your bold imagination, pioneering spirit and dynamic leadership,

In appreciation of your exceptional devotion to city, state and nation, the expression of your deep-rooted patriotism, your sense of service to your fellow man and your commitment to the ideals of freedom and justice which comprise the heritage of western civilization,

In admiration of your personal courage, loyalty and perseverance, your invariable preference for principle over expediency, and your unparalleled generosity, attributes which exemplify the spirit of that illustrious man in whose name we pay this tribute.

Presented by The Winston Churchill
Foundation of the United States

The Raoul Wallenberg Award
March 4, 1987

For tireless efforts on behalf of your fellow man;

For unmatched courage during troubled times;

For devotion to the improvement of the quality of life for all individuals;

For fortitude and conviction to act while others only watch;

In recognition of your strength of commitment to the fundamental principles of freedom;

And

For the virtues which exemplify the spirit of righteousness of the man in whose name this award is being given,

I present you with the Raoul Wallenberg Award

Presented by The Raoul Wallenberg Committee of the
United States and The American Committee
For Shaare Zedek Hospital in Jerusalem

National Business Hall of Fame Award
December 1, 1988

"Ross Perot—patriot, populist and deep believer in familial values. This successful business leader attributes his habit of 'square dealing' to his father, and his appreciation of charity's blessings to his mother. Perot's generosity has been spread over a wide variety of charities, but his most direct focus is aimed at helping underprivileged children. He often speaks with unembarrassed pride of his God, his country and his parents."

Quote from plaque presented by the
National Business Hall of Fame, December 1, 1988

Dwight D. Eisenhower Medal
1981

"In recognition of his continuing contributions to the preservation of American security, unity and world peace and his efforts in behalf of those oppressed. He won the admiration of all Americans for his actions in support of the POW/MIA in Southeast Asia."

Presented by the Veterans of Foreign Wars
Of the United States

Patrick Henry Award
May 23, 1990

Press Release
Among Mr. Perot's most well-known contributions have been his dedication to the Texas War on Drugs, his concern for American prisoners of war, and his dedication to improving the quality of education in the Texas public school system.

Joining in the tribute will be other modern day patriots—military heroes and their survivors who distinguished themselves during the 45-year cold war, including those who served in Korea, Vietnam, Europe, the Middle East, Grenada and Panama.

The director of the Patrick Henry Memorial Foundation, Mr. James Elson, stated today, "We are pleased to honor Mr. Perot, since his life, like Patrick Henry's, exemplifies courageous patriotism, high principles, and success in the private sector."

Other Comments

The Patrick Henry Memorial Foundation will salute Mr. Ross Perot for his leadership in human rights, education, the war on drugs, and, in particular, his commitment to public service and his country. Mr. Perot, not unlike Patrick Henry, embodies the spirit of American courage and patriotism.

Because of Mr. Perot's vigor and dedication to the pursuit of basic individual civil liberties, the Foundation has chosen this dinner to recognize his achievements.

Department of Defense
Medal for Distinguished Public Service
March 1, 1974

To H. Ross Perot for exceptionally meritorious service to the Department of Defense during the period December 1969 through March 1973.

During this period, Mr. Perot devoted countless hours to developing a public awareness within the international community of the plight of our captured and missing servicemen in Southeast Asia and the failure of their communist captors to adhere to the humanitarian principles of the Geneva Convention Relative to the Treatment of Prisoners of War. His use of the news media to publicize the issue was highly effective as were his personal appearances before POW/MIA family groups to inform them of his numerous activities and plans.

Mr. Perot's personal crusade on behalf of the POW/MIA took many forms. In December 1969, he sponsored a flight to Paris for over 150 family members to enable them to personally protest to the North Vietnamese delegation their failure to comply with the Geneva Convention. He also flew around the world in a widely publicized attempt to deliver Christmas packages to our men held captive in Hanoi. In April 1970, Mr.

Perot sponsored a flight for newsmen to South Vietnam to emphasize our adherence to the Geneva Convention regarding captured enemy personnel. Perhaps the most noteworthy and effective initiative by Mr. Perot resulted in the placement in the Nation's Capitol of displays portraying the rigors of captivity experienced by our men held in prison cells in North Vietnam and bamboo cages in South Vietnam.

Mr. Perot's generous and untiring efforts were highly successful in favorably influencing world opinion in behalf of our prisoners of war and missing servicemen and instrumental in serving notice to the Vietnamese communists that their nonconformity with basic humanitarian principles was not in their best interests.

It gives me great pleasure to award Mr. H. Ross Perot the Department of Defense Medal for Distinguished Public Service.

James R. Schlesinger
Secretary of Defense

The Defense Industry Award of the American Defense Preparedness Association
April 23, 1986

Ross Perot has served his country, the state of Texas, and the American people with distinction and dedication.

He graduated from the Naval Academy and saw service on a destroyer and an aircraft carrier.

He joined the business world and applied his considerable managerial talents, imagination and leadership to the computer industry.

His company of more than 40,000 employees has become the computer systems integrator for the Armed Forces.

His spectacular success in industry has been coupled with a strong belief in and concern for his fellow man.

He was instrumental in directing the world's attention to the plight of Vietnam POWs and improving their treatment.

He personally organized and supervised the rescue of two of his employees held hostage in Iran.

He has focused the attention of Texans on the war on drugs and a need for improving public education.

His complete involvement with the concerns of his country, his home state, and in matters of industrial competitiveness and excellence have earned him the respect and admiration of his fellow Americans.

The American Defense Preparedness Association is proud and honored to confer its 1986 Defense Industry Award on Ross Perot, inspired industrial leader, good citizen and patriot.

April 23, 1986
Washington, D.C.

Admiral Arleigh Burke Leadership Award
December 6, 1990

"To Ross Perot for Outstanding Leadership, Personal Integrity, Professional Achievement and Unselfish Dedication to America."

Presented by the Navy League
Of the United States